A GANNETT COMPANY

Lifeline
BIOGRAPHIES

QUEEN LATIFAH
From Jersey Girl to Superstar

by Amy Ruth Allen

TFCB

Twenty-First Century Books · Minneapolis

For Leigh, always.

Twenty-First Century Books
A division of Lerner Publishing Group, Inc.
241 First Avenue North
Minneapolis, MN 55401 U.S.A.

Website address: www.lernerbooks.com

Library of Congress Cataloging-in-Publication Data

Allen, Amy Ruth.
    Queen Latifah : from Jersey girl to superstar / by Amy Ruth Allen.
        p. cm. — (USA TODAY lifeline biographies)
    Includes bibliographical references and index.
    ISBN 978–0–7613–4234–2 (lib. bdg. : alk. paper)
    1. Latifah, Queen—Juvenile literature. 2. Rap musicians—United States—
Biography—Juvenile literature. 3. Television actors and actresses—United States—
Biography—Juvenile literature. 4. Motion picture actors and actresses—United States—
Biography—Juvenile literature. I. Title.
ML3930.L178A45 2012
782.421649092—dc23 [B]   2011021463

Manufactured in the United States of America
1 – PA – 12/31/11

≡USA TODAY. **Lifeline**
A GANNETT COMPANY   BIOGRAPHIES

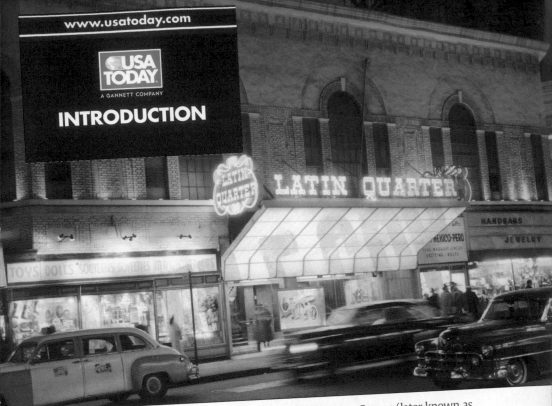

Dancing in the night: As a teenager in the mid-1980s, Dana Owens (later known as Queen Latifah) danced at the Latin Quarter nightclub in New York City. The club has been popular since the 1950s.

Unstoppable

■■■■

New York City's Latin Quarter nightclub shook with music and people. It was the mid-1980s, and the Times Square club district throbbed to the beat of rap, an exciting new sound.

Hundreds of people stood outside the Latin Quarter, eager to get inside. Onstage, rappers rhymed over music from records spinning on turntables. On the floor, throngs of dancers moved to the pulsing rhythm and chanted along with the rappers.

Dana Owens, a teenager from nearby East Orange, New Jersey, was among the dancers. To Dana, rap was more than just entertainment. With its pounding beats and bold lyrics, rap was pure drama.

Dana found the live rap scene so irresistible that she broke her curfew to experience it. After her mother and brother fell asleep, Dana sneaked out of her family's apartment to join her friends for a night of club hopping. Sometimes she took the subway into New York City. Sometimes she rode with a friend who had a car. Dana didn't care how she traveled—only that she got there.

"For my mother, it was Excedrin Headache number 9," Dana later recalled. "I was definitely too young to be going to New York City all alone and hanging out all night. Looking back on it, I say to myself, 'What were you thinking?!' I was blinded. But in truth, I do know what I was thinking. . . . I was one with this world. My blood beat to its beat. . . . I *had* to be there, and nothing

Irresistible: Dana Owens, shown here in 1989, broke her parents' curfew to go to New York City at night and experience the rap music scene there.

was going to stop me. Not even breaking my mother's heart."

Within a few years, Dana's unstoppable urge to rap had transformed her life. Barely out of high school, Dana Owens became rap superstar Queen Latifah.

Queen Latifah added a whole new dimension to the male-dominated, often vulgar and violent world of rap music. Not only was she one of very few female rappers, but she also crafted a groundbreaking style. She rapped out positive, gripping messages about racial harmony, black unity, self-respect, and female empowerment. She set standards that many later rappers—both male and female—would follow.

Queen Latifah was the first female solo rapper to sign with a major record label, and she soon became the first to earn widespread popularity. But rap was just the beginning for Queen Latifah. Since 1989 she has made eight albums and thirty movies, starred in a top-rated television series, hosted her own talk show,

Accomplished: Queen Latifah arrives at the 82nd Annual Academy Awards in 2010. She has made albums, starred in movies, and acted in television shows since her performing career began.

launched many business and charitable ventures, and won several prestigious awards.

Queen Latifah has earned worldwide admiration from people of all ages and backgrounds. Critics, politicians, journalists, and other social commentators have praised both her art and her life. Faiza Hirji, a professor of communications and media at McMaster University in Ontario, Canada, wrote, "Independent, business-savvy, and fiercely proud of her gender, her race, and her roots, Latifah brought a new sense of positivity to rap and became a role model almost instantly."

Hometown: Dana Owens was born in Newark, the largest city in New Jersey.

Dana

Dana Elaine Owens was born on March 18, 1970, in Newark, New Jersey. Her parents, Rita Bray Owens and Lancelot Owens, welcomed their daughter with relief. Dana arrived nearly one month after her due date. Her parents had grown anxious waiting for her.

"From the very beginning, I knew my daughter was going to be different," said Rita. "Dana refused to be born.... Ten long months I carried her. I finally had to tell the doctors to go in and get her. And she fought that, too. She [had] a mind of her own from day one."

Dana's big brother, Lancelot Jr., had been born two years earlier. Family and friends called him Winki. Rita had given him this nickname. As a baby, he often awoke from sleeping by opening just one eye to look at her.

Family Life

The Owens family lived in an apartment in Newark. Newark is an industrial city in eastern New Jersey, about 10 miles (16 kilometers) west of New York City.

Lancelot was a police officer. As he advanced in his career, the family moved several times. Each move brought the family to a nicer apartment in a better neighborhood. Rita was a talented artist. She filled the Owens home with beauty, books, and culture.

The whole family shared a love of music. Winki and Dana enjoyed putting on impromptu song-and-dance shows for their parents.

Family love: Queen Latifah's family is pictured in 2005. When Latifah was a child, her dad *(left)* was a police officer and her mom *(right)* was an artist.

Performing came naturally to Dana. Rita Owens recalled, "Give her a pot, she'd bang it. A spoon, she'd sing into it. A box, she'd beat it."

Music had brought Dana's parents together. Rita's father was an army sergeant stationed on a base in Arlington, Virginia. Lancelot, a young soldier who'd just returned from the Vietnam War (1957–1975), was stationed at the same base. When he was off duty, Lancelot sang with his band in the nightclub on the base. One afternoon sixteen-year-old Rita and her sister Angel came to the club and auditioned to be backup singers. Soon after they met, Lancelot asked Rita to marry him. The newlyweds settled in Newark, Lancelot's hometown.

Dana's parents worked together like musical harmony, their individual strengths complementing each other. They made a point of treating Winki and Dana similarly—a parenting style ahead of its time. In the 1970s, Americans were just beginning to view males and females as equals in society. Rita and Lancelot wanted Dana to grow up believing she could do anything. So they equipped her with self-confidence and determination.

Rita encouraged Dana to believe in herself and to pursue her dreams. And she taught both her children the importance of open, honest communication. "I [gave] my son and daughter a healthy amount of freedom . . . encouraging them to question me so that we could have a dialogue," said Rita. "I wanted Dana to feel that there was nothing she couldn't talk to me about. And there wasn't."

Strength and Self-Reliance

Lancelot taught Winki and Dana how to be physically strong and how to take care of themselves. He gave both his children lessons in firearms use and karate. "I'm not afraid of too many things," Dana said. "And I got that invincible kind of attitude from him."

Although Rita didn't like the idea of Dana handling guns or doing karate, she kept her feelings to herself. "I was afraid she would get hurt," Rita said. "But I never stopped her. . . . I was mindful not to interfere with her desires—no matter how unconventional they may have been." With her parents' constant encouragement and support, Dana's strong and lively personality blossomed. And with each challenge she met, her confidence soared. Her mother described her as a dynamo—a person with unusual energy and power.

One day in kindergarten, Dana got distracted at the end of recess. She found herself alone on the playground, locked out of the school. She knew her grandmother lived nearby. So she walked 1.5 miles (2.4 km) there. Soon she stood at Nana Owens's door, yelling for her grandma through the mail slot.

Though she was a strong and independent child, Dana cherished the comfort of friends and family. Dana and Winki were especially close. They both enjoyed the outdoors. They loved to climb trees and ride bikes together. Dana often joined Winki and his friends in their rough-and-tumble games.

When Dana fell and scraped her knees or bruised herself playing basketball, she proudly showed off her marks. "Those 'marks' were the mark of a girl unafraid," she said.

Sometimes her schoolmates teased her. They called her a tomboy, saying Dana wasn't acting the way girls should act. Dana replied, "I'm not a tomboy, I'm athletically inclined!" Her comeback earned her even more teasing—but Dana didn't care. She'd said it for her own benefit, not theirs. She wanted to remind herself that only she could define who she was.

Lancelot had learned to survive in the wild while fighting in Vietnam. He wanted his children to understand the forces of nature. So when Dana was six, Lancelot took her and Winki on their first camping trip. Rain drummed steadily all weekend. Lancelot refused to go home. Instead, he transformed the disappointment into a learning opportunity. He said, "Hey, life's not always going to be sunshine every day. What are you gonna do when there are a few clouds? You have to keep going."

IN F☉CUS

African Queens

Young Dana was fascinated with the queens of ancient Africa. These strong women had proudly ruled entire nations. Many are remembered for their strength and courage.

Ancient Egypt was a realm that flourished in northern Africa from about 3150 to 31 B.C. Ancient Egyptians revered their rulers as gods. Queen Hatshepsut ruled Egypt for two decades in the 1400s B.C. Her reign was prosperous and peaceful. She was the first woman to be buried in the Valley of the Kings, a burial site for many of ancient Egypt's important rulers and nobility. Other women, such as queens Tiye, Nefertiti, and Cleopatra, governed ancient Egypt after Hatshepsut.

Queen Amanirenas of Cush (modern Sudan) reigned from 40 to 10 B.C. She led her armies into battle against the Roman emperor Augustus.

Egyptians: The Valley of the Queens in Egypt has many statues of Queen Hatshepsut, Egypt's ruler in the 1400s B.C.

At the end of the trip, Dana was proud of her accomplishment. She'd learned to pitch a tent and start a campfire. She'd identified plants and insects. She'd used the sun and the moss on trees to get her bearings. She'd managed for several days without running water. She felt tough.

Similarly, Queen Dahia al-Kahina of the Berber people (in modern Algeria) led her soldiers against Arab invaders in the A.D. 600s.

For three decades in the A.D. 1400s or 1500s, Queen Amina ruled the kingdom of Zazzau (in modern Nigeria). She was known as a fierce warrior who greatly expanded the realm.

During the 1600s, Queen Nzinga governed the Mbundu people in southwestern Africa (modern Angola). A clever politician, Nzinga formed military alliances (partnerships) that kept her subjects safe from Portuguese slave traders for thirty years.

In 1900 Queen Yaa Asantewa defended her land against a different group of Europeans. She led the Ashanti people of Ghana, a country in western Africa, into battle against British colonists.

Under the leadership of such brave and wise female rulers, some of the world's early civilizations flourished. Stories, poems, and songs telling of African queens' courage, intelligence, and beauty passed from generation to generation. Centuries after these queens lived, their descendants honored them by recording their stories in writing.

Mbundu people: Queen Nzinga governed her people in southwestern Africa in the 1600s.

Focus on Learning

Education was just as important in Dana's family as strength and self-reliance were. Dana and Winki attended private school. Rita and Lancelot believed private schooling was worth the expense, because it reinforced the values of hard work, discipline, and self-respect that they taught their children at home.

For the Owens family, self-respect included pride in their heritage. Rita and Lancelot taught their children to respect their African roots. They introduced Dana and Winki to African culture and history.

Even the family's leisure time included learning. Rita brought books along on picnics and visits to the park. She used them to teach her children about science and math.

This focus on learning paid off. By second grade, officials at Dana's school identified her as gifted, and she skipped a grade.

Harmony

For Dana and Winki, early childhood was a happy

The Huxtables: Dana Owens thought her family was very similar to the Huxtable family on *The Cosby Show*. This sitcom was about an African American family in Brooklyn, New York.

time. Latifah compared her family to the fictional Huxtable family, made famous by the television program *The Cosby Show* (1984–1992). The Owens household dished out plenty of hugs and daily doses of praise and encouragement. Lancelot loved roughhousing with his kids after work and on his days off. The house sang with the sounds of jazz, soul, and rock-and-roll music. On Sundays the family attended church, where Dana fell in love with the rich sounds of gospel music.

"We had a lot of love and laughter in our house," Latifah said. "We had a lot of jokes and a lot of quality time. My brother and I didn't have a care in the world."

Ravaged town: Two children walk home from school over battered sidewalks in Newark in 1972. Riots in the 1960s left Dana's New Jersey hometown weakened economically.

Latifah

The late 1970s brought two big changes to Dana's carefree life. In 1978 she both gained a new name and lost her tight-knit family.

A New Name

Many African Americans took Muslim names in the 1970s. (Muslims are followers of the religion of Islam.) They did so as a symbol of their pride and determination to overcome social injustices.

Several of Dana's friends and relatives assumed Muslim names. But Dana hadn't considered doing so until her Muslim cousin Sharonda Mamoud

Muslims believe that Allah (God) gave messages to the prophet Muhammad through the angel Gabriel in the A.D. 600s. The Quran contains these messages. Muslims strive to declare their faith, pray five times daily, give charity, fast during the holy month of Ramadan, and travel to the holy city of Mecca, Saudi Arabia, once in a lifetime.

suggested it. One day when Dana was eight years old, the two girls were hanging out together. Sharonda excitedly showed Dana a book of Muslim names and their meanings. Sharonda had chosen the name Salima Wadiah, meaning "healthy and peaceful."

Dana read through the names carefully, wanting to find a perfect fit. "I knew then that something as simple as picking a new name for myself would be my first act of defining who I was—for myself and for the world," she recalled.

Choosing a name: Many African Americans, including Dana Owens, took Muslim names in the 1970s. Some Muslim names come from the Quran *(above)*, the holy book of Islam.

IN FOCUS

Why Muslim Names?

In the 1950s and 1960s, many African Americans participated in the civil rights movement. This movement was a long series of nonviolent protests for racial equality. It succeeded in changing U.S. laws to end legal racial discrimination.

But the changes in law did not change reality. The United States continued to be racially segregated (separated) in many ways—especially in access to good jobs, health care, education, and housing.

In the late 1960s, African Americans were still struggling for a fair shake. Most could find only low-paying jobs. Black professionals earned less money for performing the same

Marching for equality: Martin Luther King Jr. *(front left)* walks with others during the March on Washington for Jobs and Freedom in 1963. This event was a rally in support of equal rights for African Americans.

duties as their white colleagues. Many African Americans lived in poor, run-down neighborhoods and found that they were unwelcome elsewhere. Few politicians in local, state, and national government were sympathetic to the plight of blacks.

The future looked bleak. Crime, hopelessness, and unemployment mounted in U.S. cities. Several times, frustrated and angry black youths and adults rioted upon hearing news or rumors of police brutality against blacks. They wanted their white neighbors and lawmakers to know that they were fed up.

The riots subsided in the 1970s. African Americans looked for ways to rebuild their broken communities.

Many turned to the Nation of Islam, a religion founded to improve the lives of African Americans. Its leaders, such as Malcolm X, inspired many people with their message of black superiority. The Nation of Islam offered a positive alternative to unemployment, hopelessness, and crime. It provided spiritual and cultural fellowship for African Americans. It encouraged them to take pride in themselves.

Most black Americans did not join the Nation of Islam. But they took its message of black pride to heart. Many African Americans—Muslim or not—demonstrated their pride by taking Muslim names to replace their

Pride: Malcolm X speaks during a rally in 1964. Malcolm X was a Nation of Islam leader.

European American names. They described their European American names as slave names.

Islam is a common religion in Africa. Up to 20 percent of early African Americans may have been Muslims. Slavery largely destroyed this heritage. However, many recent African immigrants to the United States practice Islam. For these reasons, many blacks identify with Muslim culture.

When she came to the name Latifah, Dana said it out loud, letting the sounds roll off her tongue. She liked how the name sounded, and she really liked what it meant. "'Delicate, sensitive, kind' accurately described exactly who I was inside. . . . I loved how it made me feel—feminine and special. The people in my world may have been perceiving me as something else, but . . . I knew who I was inside, and I wanted to show a bit of that on the outside."

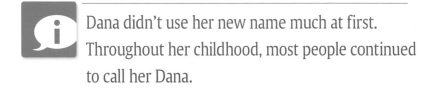

Dana didn't use her new name much at first. Throughout her childhood, most people continued to call her Dana.

Dana's choice confirmed what Rita had always known about her daughter. Dana loved sports and hated dresses, was big for her age, and fought boys without fear. But "Dana's daintiness was internal," Rita said. "She had softness and gentleness. They were very much a part of my daughter's character. If you told Dana she had disappointed you, she would shed tears. She was, above all, sensitive. . . . My daughter was strong on the outside, but soft as a down pillow on the inside."

Family Breakup

Dana's sensitivity made it hard for her to cope with the next major event of 1978: her parents' separation. Family had always been important to both of Dana's parents. However, their shared values couldn't help Lancelot overcome his personal problems.

As a soldier and a police officer, Lancelot had been shot at many times and had killed several people in the line of duty. He had difficulty coming to terms with his experiences. Memories of the terrors he'd faced and the lives he'd ended tormented him. His superiors never offered him counseling for his troubles, and he couldn't deal with them on his own. Lancelot became depressed. He turned to other women for comfort. He used drugs to numb his pain and became addicted to cocaine.

Cocaine affects the central nervous system, providing temporary pleasure. But the drug stresses vital organs, such as the heart and the lungs, and eventually poisons the body. When the high (pleasurable feeling) wears off, the user craves more cocaine and may become paranoid (suspicious of others) and violent.

Rita still loved Lancelot. But to keep herself and her children safe—both phys-

Split: Queen Latifah's parents separated in 1978. Her mother *(left)* raised both children on her own. Rita and Latifah are pictured here at an awards ceremony in 1991.

ically and emotionally—Rita decided to leave her husband. "We could not imagine that we would no longer be a family," Dana recalled. "I didn't understand what was happening. I just knew we were leaving."

Dana and Winki both struggled with the painful news. For a time, sadness, anger, and doubt masked Dana's happy, confident personality. Though she understood the importance of communication, she had trouble expressing her emotions. "Dana became very aggressive and very defiant," Rita said. "She wasn't able to vocalize her hurt until much later."

New home: The Owens family lived for two years in a housing project in Newark, New Jersey, similar to the one shown above. Newark's projects housed several thousand low-income residents.

Hyatt Court

Rita and Lancelot's separation brought quick and drastic changes to Dana's life. Lancelot moved out of the family's apartment. Lancelot couldn't work and provided the family with little financial help, so money was tight. Rita could not afford the rent on her own.

Rita had no choice but to move with Dana and Winki to Hyatt Court, a government-supported apartment complex on Newark's east side. In the United States, public housing developments such as Hyatt Court are commonly known as the projects.

Troubled Newark

When Rita, Winki, and Dana moved to Hyatt Court in 1978, it was one of many run-down neighborhoods in Newark. The city had lost 20 percent of its population in the 1960s and the 1970s. Most of its once-thriving industry had fled too. Newark was full of barren landscapes.

The year 1967 had been especially bad. On the night of July 12, white police officers stopped a black cabdriver for a minor traffic violation. They arrested him, beat him, and brought him to a police station. Black residents of an apartment complex across the street watched the officers drag the cabdriver inside. When he failed to reappear, rumors spread that police had beaten him to death. (Actually, they'd taken him to a hospital at the insistence of civil rights leaders.) Rioters spilled into the streets. They smashed windows, looted stores, and burned entire city blocks to the ground.

On the third day of rioting, National Guard soldiers, who were trained to respond quickly to local emergencies, arrived in Newark. Eventually nearly thirty-five hundred troops arrived. Their presence sparked even more violence.

The rioting ended on July 17. About fifteen hundred people had been wounded, sixteen hundred arrested, and twenty-six people killed. Twenty-four of the dead were black. Investigators later concluded that panicky soldiers had killed many innocent bystanders.

After the riots, middle-class residents left Newark even faster than they had before. They took with them their tax dollars, which had helped pay for schools and other public services. The city spiraled into despair.

Newark's recovery was excruciatingly slow. The city's crime rate and unemployment remained high into the 21st century.

Rioters: Firefighters spray water onto burning buildings caused by riots in Newark on July 14, 1967.

Rita promised her kids that their stay in the projects was temporary.

Dana tried not to get discouraged. But she couldn't help remembering how her family used to pile in the car and drive around Newark's rich neighborhoods, imagining life in a fancy mansion. "Until then, our family had always been moving to a better place and a better neighborhood . . . ," she said, "but this time, it wasn't a step up, and Daddy wasn't there."

Not of the Projects

Hyatt Court is a group of several brick apartment buildings built around a series of courtyards, which serve as social gathering places. Rita, Winki, and Dana moved into unit 3K of their building, an apartment on the third floor.

Even though Rita intended Hyatt Court to be a brief stop on the way to a better place, she carefully transformed the apartment into

While Dana was coping with family upheaval, the world around her was also in tumult. In the 1970s, Americans of all backgrounds voiced their concerns about the environment and discrimination (unfair treatment) against women and racial minorities. Music was an important form of activism during this time, as it had been in others. Many bands of the 1970s sang about personal, political, and social issues.

a comfortable home. "My mother wanted 3K to feel like our space," Dana said. "With so much change in our young lives, she knew just how extra important it was for us to feel comfortable and safe."

Dana and Winki each had their own room. Dana made hers a sanctuary—a place where she could be alone with her thoughts. She arranged the furniture to create an open area where she could dance to her favorite music, such as the Jackson 5, the Delfonics, and Jamaican reggae. Listening to familiar tunes helped her adjust to her new home.

The Owens apartment was a bright spot in a bleak housing complex. Dana described Hyatt Court as a "barren landscape." Garbage often littered the courtyards and hallways. Grime and

Pop hits: Growing up, Dana Owens liked to dance to music by groups such as the Jackson 5, pictured here in 1977.

soot caked the stairways. Graffiti covered the walls, outside and inside. Kids and adults—many unemployed—hung out on their stoops. Loud music and loud voices filled the air.

Rita made it clear that the family would be moving on as soon as possible. "You may live in the projects, but you're not *of* the projects," she told Winki and Dana. Dana and Winki were anxious to leave Hyatt Court too.

Rita worked hard to make it happen. She toiled at a Newark post office through the night, while her kids slept. When her shift ended at seven in the morning, she dashed home to make breakfast and take Dana and Winki to school. Then she went to her second job waiting tables at the Holiday Inn. She got off at two o'clock and picked up her kids from school. They went home to make dinner and spend the evening together. Rita was determined to not only provide for her family's daily needs but also to keep sending her kids to private school. And she didn't just want to move out of the projects, she wanted to buy a house. She saved every penny she could.

Rita also revived her childhood dream of becoming a trained artist. She enrolled in Kean University, just outside Newark. Taking classes part-time in the evenings, she studied to become an art teacher. On class nights, Dana and Winki joined their mother on campus.

Before Rita met Lancelot, she had planned to attend college. She'd received acceptance letters from Howard University in Washington, D.C., and Spelman College in Atlanta, Georgia. But she postponed college to be a wife and mother.

When they weren't at school or with their mother, Dana and Winki avoided the Hyatt Court courtyard and the kids who hung out there. Dana explained, "It wasn't enough for us to just hang out in the courtyard. Instead of finding trouble on the streets, we were more interested in *fun*." They spent hours together playing board games and Ping-Pong at the recreation center across the street. With similar interests and few friends in the neighborhood, brother and sister grew even closer.

Summer in the South

When school let out for the summer, Hyatt Court exploded with restless young people. The sun beat down on the city, trapping the heat in the streets, sidewalks, and buildings. But that didn't keep kids from crowding into the courtyards, looking for something to do. Sometimes they spent entire days just hanging around, not doing anything. Many got into trouble selling drugs on nearby street corners.

Rita wanted to keep Dana and Winki out of this environment, so she sent them to visit her family in Virginia. There the long, sultry (hot and humid) summer days were filled with family, wholesome fun, and a sense of peace. Grandma Bray's yard had trees for Dana and Winki to climb and large green spaces for them to play in. Dana loved experiencing nature, which was hard to do in Newark. She enjoyed breathing the clean air, watching the birds, and feeling the soft grass tickle her bare feet.

Family fun: During the summer, Rita *(left)* sent her kids to Virginia to stay with her mother, Katherine *(center)*. This kept them away from the hazards of Hyatt Court. Rita, Katherine, and Latifah are pictured here in 2003.

"There our life slowed down and was cleaned up," Dana remembered. "We ate from fruit bushes and pecan trees that we climbed. There were pools with clean water where there weren't a thousand kids crammed in to get a splash like at Newark's pools. People smiled and had manners. . . . And every meal seemed like Thanksgiving."

Summer vacation in Virginia provided something else Dana loved—an appreciative audience. Rita came from a family of seven children, so Dana and Winki had plenty of aunts, uncles, and cousins in the South. Dana had fun showing them her musical and theatrical skills. She delighted her relatives with her talent for mimicking people she heard on television and radio. She especially enjoyed doing Jamaican, French, and Spanish accents.

"She liked to be in the spotlight, where people would look at her and laugh," remembered Dana's grandmother, Katherine Bray.

Dana's aunt Angel was impressed with her niece's talent and tenacity (determination). "She was the go-getter," she said. "She always aspired to do, and she did."

Onward and Upward

Although Rita worked hard to create a good life for her children, they still felt a void. Dana and Winki missed their dad. And even though they knew better, they couldn't help worrying that they'd done something to drive him away. While Lancelot struggled to overcome his drug dependence, "Winki, my mom, and I suffered with him—and for him," Dana recalled.

Meanwhile, Lancelot also tried to maintain a relationship with his children. Dana and Winki enjoyed the times when their father treated them to a Chinese dinner and led them in karate exercises. Although they saw much less of their father after the separation, they knew he loved them. "At least he was still around; he was never far away," Latifah said. "When I called him, he was there."

After one year in Hyatt Court, Rita had saved enough money for a down payment on a house. (The down payment was part of the full price, so Rita would have to pay the rest later.) She took Dana and Winki house hunting, and the three fell in love with a blue house set in a small yard. But when Rita applied for a loan to buy the house, the bank denied her. At that time, most banks wouldn't loan money to a divorced woman or to a woman with no credit history (a history of borrowing money and successfully repaying it). Many banks also discriminated against African Americans.

Rita was determined to keep her promise to leave Hyatt Court. So she rented a house on Littleton Avenue, in a pleasant section of Newark. Dana loved the big, airy rooms in her new home. But its best feature was the big backyard. After an uncomfortable year, Dana was back in a safe, quiet neighborhood. She regained the sense of security and progress that she'd lost when her family moved to Hyatt Court.

CHAPTER FOUR

Academics: In 1984 Dana Owens entered Irvington High School in suburban Newark. She was a good student and was involved in many extracurricular activities.

Birth of a Rapper

■■■■■

Dana waited nervously backstage in the auditorium of Saint Anne School. The seventh grader had landed the lead role in the musical *The Wiz*. She was about to make her stage debut (first appearance) to an audience packed with classmates, teachers, friends, and parents. Rita, Winki, and other relatives waited anxiously for the curtain to rise.

Finally, Dana stepped onstage. For the rest of the evening, she moved the audience with her strong, clear voice. When she sang the song "Home," the audience gave her a standing ovation. Rita and Winki were astonished. They knew Dana loved singing—but they had not realized just how talented she was.

"I had never heard her sing like that before," Rita remembered. "People were crying."

Irvington High

In 1984 Dana made the leap from Saint Anne to Irvington High School in Irvington, a suburb west of Newark. Dana was already familiar with her new school. Her mother had taken a job as an art teacher there after finishing her college degree.

Around the same time, the family moved to an apartment in East Orange, another suburb nearby. Despite her outgoing nature, Dana always felt a little shy when she moved to a new neighborhood.

She perked up when she met Mondo, a high school senior. Mondo became her first boyfriend. He treated Dana with respect, and she liked that. In the years since her parents' split, Dana had learned about the troubles in Rita and Lancelot's marriage. She was shocked to discover that Lancelot had fathered three children with other women. The news left Dana feeling confused and distrustful. Mondo helped her sort through her emotions. He soon left for college, but Dana kept in touch with him.

Dana quickly fell in love with Irvington High. She participated eagerly in many academic and extracurricular activities.

Dana was a good student. She loved writing and reading poems. She also enjoyed debating with her friends about racism, drugs, and South Africa's apartheid (laws that separated whites from others and discriminated against nonwhites, 1948–1994). After high school, Dana hoped to earn a broadcast journalism degree or maybe even become a lawyer.

She lost no time joining the Irvington music scene. A big fan of reggae bands, the Jackson 5, and Patti LaBelle, Dana seemed to be

In black poet and civil rights activist Nikki Giovanni, Dana found a strong voice much like her own. "Nikki's poems struck me. I could feel her," Dana said. "I liked her play on words and how she threw a little rhythm around. All her poetry seemed to be real and to have love in it. It was based on the fact that she cared about herself and about black people."

Impact: In high school, Dana Owens was influenced by poet Nikki Giovanni (above). Giovanni, seen here in 1973, focused on the power an individual has to make a difference.

singing all the time. She won the school's talent show during her first year there, singing "If Only for One Night," a love song by Luther Vandross.

Dana was not only a talented performer but also a star athlete. The same year she won the school talent show, the girls' basketball team stomped its rivals all the way to the state championship. As a forward, Dana helped her team win the state title.

She made lots of new friends at Irvington High. Tammy Hammond, a fellow basketball star, became Dana's best friend. The two often hung out together at Tammy's house, which overflowed with activity.

Baller: Dana Owens played forward on the Irvington High School basketball team and helped her team win the state championship during her sophomore year.

Dana's self-confidence and high standards rubbed off on those around her. For example, she learned that a boy in her geometry class, Shakim Compere, had a crush on her. She explained to him that she couldn't date him because he had several bad habits, including smoking and cutting class. Pretty soon, Shakim dropped those habits. He and Dana became close friends, often studying together.

"I knew from the start that he had the makings of a true friend. And true friends hold each other accountable [responsible]," Dana said. "He trusted me, because I was honest with him from the beginning."

Although Dana had many friends at Irvington, she still counted on her brother for advice and support. Winki never let her down. As a teenager, he dipped into his wages from his after-school job to give Dana a weekly allowance. In exchange, she cleaned his room and ironed his clothes. "Winki was the one constant friend in my life," Dana said.

IN F⊕CUS

Hip-Hop Roots

Disc jockeys (DJs) in the Bronx, one of the five boroughs that make up New York City, laid the foundations of hip-hop. Many people credit DJ Kool Herc (Clive Campbell) with inventing hip-hop in the mid-1970s.

At parties and dances that he hosted throughout the Bronx, Campbell noticed that dancers would go wild during the break in each song—the brief part during which the band drops out and the rhythm section takes over. So he used two copies of the same record. As one record reached the end of a break, he switched to the other record, playing it at the beginning of the break. Using this method, Campbell could extend a five-second break into a "five-minute loop of fury." Soon he abandoned all but the breaks. He called the dancers at his events break-dancers, or b-boys and b-girls.

Foundations: Many people credit DJ Kool Herc *(left)* for inventing hip-hop. He is pictured here in 1999 with DJ Grandmaster Flash.

"Not only was he the man of the house after my parents split up, but he was also my protector and my soul mate."

Ladies Fresh

As teenagers Winki and Dana were drawn to the bold rhythms and lyrics of the latest U.S. musical trend, rap. Rap caught on slowly at Ir-

As Campbell gained popularity, he started playing in Bronx nightclubs. He was a Jamaican immigrant, so he introduced the Jamaican tradition of toasting to the clubs. When Jamaican DJs toasted, they spoke abbreviated words and sentences over music. A toast often boasted of the DJ's talents and accomplishments.

Theodore Livingston was another Bronx DJ who developed a key element of hip-hop. Livingston called himself Grand Wizard Theodore. He invented scratching, the technique of moving a playing record back and forth rhythmically beneath the record-player needle.

Joseph Saddler, yet another Bronx DJ, called himself Grandmaster Flash. He perfected and popularized scratching. He also added rappers to his nightclub routine. Some people called rappers MCs (masters of ceremonies), or emcees. While Saddler mixed the music, his rappers spoke or chanted rhyming lyrics to keep the audience dancing.

Rappers drew on centuries-old African music and storytelling traditions, modern African American street slang, and civil rights sentiments to express themselves. As rappers vied for admiration from hip-hop fans and fellow rappers, rap became very competitive.

Stand up: Grand Wizard Theodore invented scratching to create a unique sound.

vington High, so Dana gravitated toward those who shared her interest. One fellow rap lover was Ramsey Gbelawoe. Ramsey introduced her to hip-hop gear (clothing and jewelry), which he bought in New York City boutiques. (Hip-hop is the category of music to which rap belongs, as well as the culture surrounding it.)

Ramsey was an older high school student with his own apartment.

The sound: Dana Owens enjoyed going out to New York City clubs to see famous hip-hop performers such as Run-D.M.C., pictured here in 1988.

Dana began hanging out there, enjoying the freedom to listen to rap and talk about it for hours. Ramsey and his friends took Dana to rap clubs in New York City to experience live performances. Soon she was going clubbing as often as she could. She saw famous acts such as Grandmaster Flash, Doug E. Fresh, and Run-D.M.C. She reveled in the sights and sounds of hip-hop culture.

"I was attracted to the sound and the content and the freedom of rap," Latifah said. "To me, it's like a free art form. It flows. It's smooth. It can be anything you want it to be."

Dana and Winki often decked themselves out in hip-hop gear:

baggy pants and shirts, hooded sweatshirts, leather jackets, and un-laced sneakers. Dana took a job at Burger King to pay for hip-hop al-bums and clothes. She practiced rapping whenever she could. During basketball season, her coach often suggested, "Dana, give us a little rap and cheer us up."

She even started her own rap group, called Ladies Fresh. She wrote her own lyrics, drawing on memories and lessons from her childhood. "Being Afrocentric and proud of my heritage, that's something I grew up with," Latifah said. "My mother always taught me that. When I started rapping, I wanted to make it part of my image."

Ladies Fresh performances lit up the Irvington auditorium and en-ergized fans at basketball games. For a while, the trio was the only female rap group at Irvington High. Then another girls' group chal-lenged Ladies Fresh to a rap throwdown, daring the trio to prove their superiority. The competition inspired Dana and her friends.

"We stayed up all night writing stuff," Dana remembered, "and I haven't stopped since."

The Flavor Unit

Rita Owens didn't realize how obsessed with rap her daughter was. But ironically, Rita was the one who sent Dana down the path to stardom.

Rita was responsible for choosing the entertainment for Irvington High events. "I knew not to get a square [old-fashioned and boring] DJ but one who really pumped it," Rita said. "I heard Mark James play for another class and I just loved what he did." Mark was a popular New Jersey disc jockey known as DJ Mark the 45 King. She hired him to spin and mix records at a school dance.

Dana and Mark hit it off right away. Like Ramsey, Mark was a few years older than Dana. He had a place of his own. His basement was filled with turntables and mixing equipment. Dana hung out at Mark's house, which was close to Irvington High, almost every afternoon.

So did many other young people who wanted to rap to Mark's mixing. Ramsey usually stopped by. Shakim, Dana's study buddy, also

Reading material: Janet Jackson is pictured on the cover of *Right On!* magazine in 1984. Dana Owens read about hip-hop in magazines like this one.

became a regular fixture in Mark's basement. Anthony Teaks (Apache) and his little brother Latee, Larry Welsh (Lakim Shabazz), Robert Frazier (Chill Rob G), and Kurtis Addison (Lord Alibaski) did too. This crew of rappers called themselves the Flavor Unit. In hip-hop slang, *flavor* or *flava* means "unique."

At first Dana was a little unsure of herself. Hanging back, she listened to Mark's collection of rap albums and devoured issues of the first hip-hop magazines *Right On!* and *Word Up!* "[I] studied rap inside and out," Latifah recalled. "It was like the training before the job."

The rappers in the Flavor Unit taught and mentored Dana. Ramsey emerged as the group's leader. He believed strongly in the Flavor Unit. He encouraged and motivated everyone with his vision and expectations. He even spent his own money to advance his friends' music careers.

Record companies and radio disc jockeys were always on the lookout for new talent. Each year they received thousands of demo tapes (demonstration recordings) from hopeful musicians. If disc jockeys liked what they heard, they played it on the air. Record company executives might sign recording contracts with musicians they liked.

To get the attention of record producers and radio DJs, the Flavor Unit rappers needed to make demo tapes. Recording a demo tape required a recording studio. Renting a recording studio was expensive. So the Flavor Unit rappers practiced in Mark's basement until they were sure they could make a demo in just a few hours.

Ramsey often used his rent money to pay for recording sessions at a nearby studio. "We were broke kids but we had a lot of big dreams," Dana recalled.

Princess of the Posse

With prodding from Ramsey, Dana soon shed her shyness. She called herself the Princess of the Posse because she was the youngest member and only girl in the Flavor Unit. She started rapping for her friends. She improvised, letting the beat of the music draw out her rhymes on the spot. This type of rap, called freestyling, is difficult. But Dana was up to the challenge.

"I knew that I had it in me. I could hear in my head the way I wanted to sound," she said. "It was just a matter of getting it from my brain to my voice."

After mixing songs in Mark's basement, the Flavor Unit rappers hit the streets to scope out the competition. They went to block parties and nightclubs in New Jersey and New York City. Sometimes Dana stayed out until the wee hours, slipping back into her bedroom in time to catch a few hours of sleep before school.

Dana felt bad about hiding her outings from her mother. But she knew Rita worried about violence, and Dana didn't want to add to her distress. "Every weekend there was a major brawl," Dana said about the club scene. "I'd watch somebody get robbed, then the bouncers would come in and tear the club up. It was like a ritual."

Dana and her friends often headed to the Latin Quarter, a hip-hop club in the seedy Times Square district of New York City. In the mid-1980s, the Latin Quarter was popular among teens. It allowed teens

IN F⊙CUS

Early Female Rappers

One of the first female rappers was Lolita Shanté Gooden. Gooden wrote her first rap in response to the group UTFO's women-bashing rap, "Roxanne, Roxanne." She called it "Roxanne's Revenge" and recorded it in 1984 under the name Roxanne Shanté.

Soon other female rappers emerged to challenge their male counterparts. MC Lyte and Sparky D (Doreen Broadnax) rapped about relationships, family and personal problems, and the difficult choices women face. Rappers Shazzy (Sherry Raquel Marsh) and Yo-Yo (Yolanda Whittaker) also tackled serious social issues.

Females step up: Roxanne Shanté, pictured here in 1988, was one of the first famous female rappers.

to enter the club but did not serve them alcohol. With its black walls, many dance floors, and strobe lights, the Latin Quarter drew the hottest rappers of the day. Dana and her posse danced to the live music of Kool Moe Dee (Mohandas Dewese) and the group Run-D.M.C. Female rapper MC Lyte (Lana Michelle Moorer) and the first major female rap group, Salt 'n' Pepa, also appeared at the Latin Quarter.

"When I came onto the scene, rap was entering a new phase," Dana said. "The consciousness movement was emerging. It was not just simple rhymes over the most popular songs; the music was about saying something. . . . And simply by being there, I was one of the

A force: Kool Moe Dee performs onstage around 1990. Dana Owens danced to his music at the Latin Quarter.

people making the culture. It was amazing to be a part of such a force."

Rap was no longer a single type of music. New styles were developing. They included lightweight pop rap, Afrocentric rap, and hard-core gangsta rap. (Gangsta rap portrays the violence and drug use of urban gang life in explicit language. It often expresses hostility toward white people, women, and authority figures.)

During a hip-hop performance at the Latin Quarter one night, Dana began seriously considering a future as a rapper. Few female rappers existed in 1986. Those who did break into the male-dominated scene wore skimpy outfits and looked like models. Dana had little in common with them. Still athletic, Dana wore comfortable clothes and kept her hair cropped short or pulled into a ponytail. A performance by Sweet Tee and DJ Jazzy Joyce gave her additional confidence. They tore up the stage at the Latin Quarter with their masterful mixes and casual but assured stage presence.

"They were just regular girls in their Adidas sweat suits. . . . Not a lot of glitz, just straight-up hip-hop," Dana said. "For the first time, I saw the possibilities. I saw someone who looked like me doing something I'd only imagined doing. Before [I saw them], it had never really occurred to me that I could be up there, rocking the house."

While exploring the world of hip-hop, Dana was also enjoying a busy senior year at Irvington High. She continued to rule the basketball court. A 5-foot 10-inch (1.8-meter) powerhouse of speed and precision, Dana led her team to another state championship, scoring the winning point with just one second left in the game. At the end of the school year, the class of 1987 voted Dana Best All Around, Most Popular, Most Comical, and Best Dancer in Irvington's senior class poll.

Well liked: Dana Owens graduated from high school in 1987. Her classmates named her Best All Around, Most Popular, Most Comical, and Best Dancer.

From Demo to Deal

After graduating from high school, Dana decided to study broadcast journalism at the Borough of Manhattan Community College in New York City. She began classes that summer.

She also kept dreams of a music career in the back of her mind. She considered her options. Perhaps her raps could take her somewhere. Maybe she could get a song on the radio. She had to try.

With seven hundred dollars from Ramsey, Dana rented time at

a small studio the summer after graduation. She was determined to record a demo tape. Mark would help her with the production, and she'd call herself Latifah. She rapped an introduction, "Greetings I Bring from La," and two songs, "Wrath of My Madness" and "Princess of the Posse."

"From the start, my style was different," Latifah said. "I sang the intro and rapped in a Jamaican dialect. Nobody was doing that back then." She had a demo tape in hand a couple of hours later. Dana and Mark exchanged smiles. "We knew it was good," Dana said.

They were right. One evening a few weeks later, Dana was listening to the radio in her family's kitchen. She heard the opening lines of "Princess of the Posse."

"My record. My song. Me. Playing on the radio. I was so excited . . . I just ran to the window and screamed out, 'My record is on the radio! My record is on the radio!'" Dana said. And the news was about to get even better.

Mark had given Dana's demo to Fab 5 Freddy (Fred Braithwaite), host of *Yo! MTV Raps*, a program on Music Television (MTV). Freddy liked what he

Television power: Fab 5 Freddy poses for a photo around 1990. He received Dana Owens's demo tape when he was the host of *Yo! MTV Raps*.

heard from this unknown New Jersey teen. Her lyrics and sound were different. Her character, too, was different from any other rapper he'd heard. "She had a dignity and a kind of regal quality and street sense [but] was feminine and womanly at the same time," Braithwaite remembered.

Braithwaite gave Dana's demo to Tommy Boy Records, a label known for signing rap artists. Dana caught the attention of Tommy Boy president Monica Lynch. A few days after hearing her song on the radio, Dana was playing basketball outside her apartment. She came in after the game and heard the phone ringing. She picked it up. It was Lynch on the line, wanting to talk about a record contract.

Dana handled the opportunity skillfully. She met with Tommy Boy executives to discuss the terms of the contract. "She impressed everyone," Lynch remembered. "You could tell she was something special."

"It was frightening because it happened so quickly," Rita remembered. "Tommy Boy was calling the house and two days later we signed on the dotted line."

Rap label: Tommy Boy Records executive Monica Lynch, seen here in 1992, heard Dana Owens's demo and gave her a record deal.

Girl power: Salt 'n' Pepa pose for a photo in 1988. They were some of only a few women to make it big as rap artists.

Dana's passion and dedication were about to pay off. "Becoming . . . a rapper didn't just happen overnight," she said. "Subconsciously I had been preparing for it most of my life. The music lessons. The talent shows. All those nights at the clubs, the endless hours in DJ Mark the 45 King's basement, the practicing, the reading, prepared me for something."

But she remained cautious. She knew how difficult it was to make a career as a rapper—especially for a woman. Roxanne Shanté, MC Lyte, Salt 'n' Pepa, and a few others had broken into the industry, but their accomplishments didn't guarantee success for Dana. She wasn't about to gamble her whole future. Dana decided that for the time being, she would pursue a music career while staying in college. "I was raised to always have something to fall back on," she said.

USA TODAY

Life

SECTION D

LIFE.USATODAY.COM

February 5, 1990

Top female entries in the rap race

From the Pages of
USA TODAY

Salt 'n' Pepa are still arguably rap's top women. But since their 1½-year hiatus [break], hot competition has emerged:

- Queen Latifah. The so-called Aretha Franklin of rap is the hottest newcomer. Her debut, *All Hail the Queen* (Tommy Boy), is a smorgasbord that embraces soul, house music, reggae and funk horns, all topped with her machine-gun-style rap. The East Orange, N.J., native (Latifah Owens), 19, aims to cross over with dance-floor-targeted cuts like "Dance for Me," based on Sly & the Family Stone's hit "Dance to the Music," and "Mama Gave Birth to the Soul Children," where she's joined by rap buddies and label mates De La Soul. Though she avoids profanity, she boasts like male rappers.
- MC Lyte. Unlike Latifah, Lyte (Lana Moorer), 19, uses four-letter words freely, and her raps take a grimmer look at life. She emerged three years ago with the song "I Cram to Understand U," about a woman who discovers her boyfriend is a crack addict. On her latest LP, *Eyes on This* (First Priority/Atlantic), she expounds on drugs ("Cappuccino"), drug pushers ("Not Wit' a Dealer") and women's rights ("I'm Not Having It").
- Roxanne Shanté. Dubbed the first lady of rap, Roxanne Shanté (Lolita Gooden) from Long Island, N.Y., got her start five years ago at 14, attracting national attention with "Roxanne's Revenge"—one of a slew of recordings that responded to UTFO's hit "Roxanne, Roxanne." *Bad Sister* (Cold Chillin'/Warner Bros.) is her first LP. It contains the usual boastings, along with hilarious, sometimes risqué stories.

—James T. Jones IV

Big name: Queen Latifah, seen here in 1990, added the "Queen" in front of Latifah after signing with Tommy Boy Records. She performed with a "crown" to show her pride in her African heritage.

The Queen Has Arrived

▬▬▬◼

Dana had recorded her demo tape under the name Latifah, but she wasn't quite satisfied with that name. She wanted a stage name that would grab people's attention. She considered calling herself MC Latifah. But she knew that would make her just another MC. To distinguish herself from other rappers, she needed a unique name—one that represented her personal values.

She thought back through her life for inspiration. She remembered her conversations with friends and family about apartheid in

South Africa and about racial injustice in the United States. She remembered the times when her parents had proudly told her about her African heritage. She remembered the strong women in her life, such as her grandmothers and aunts. Dana especially wanted to honor her mother. "In many ways, she was the queen who gave me the guts and the confidence to become one myself," Dana said.

So Dana Owens became Queen Latifah. She chose the name "not to denote rank, but to acknowledge that all black people come from a long line of kings and queens that they've never known about. This is my way of giving tribute to them," she said.

The Message in the Music

Latifah wanted her music to stand out, just as her name did. Men dominated early rap. They often portrayed women negatively, and their lyrics boasted of violence, sex, and abuse. Latifah hoped to offer an alternative to the graphic, vulgar lyrics of most male rappers.

The message: Gangsta rappers, including the N.W.A. *(pictured)*, wrote lyrics that degraded women and glorified violence and promiscuous sex.

June 17, 1994

A balance of understanding and censorship

<u>From the Pages of</u>
<u>USA TODAY</u>

Not since rock 'n' roll has a genre of music perplexed parents as much as gangsta rap. The genre is particularly disconcerting to black fathers who can empathize, but not always agree, with some of the explicit, street-oriented nature of its lyrics.

"Rap is a form of poetry and a way of communicating different messages of today's youth," writes Salestus Winkley, 36, Dallas [Texas]. But "as a parent, I have a problem with their method of expression."

Winkley was among 154 black fathers who wrote to USA TODAY about the special challenges they face. Eight came to USA TODAY headquarters in Arlington, Va., for a panel discussion that ranged from racism to parental discipline.

But the debate heated up over the misogynistic [anti-woman] and violent lyrics dominating some of gangsta rap today.

"I don't allow my daughter to watch (the videos) because I don't like the image that they portray of women," says Andre Murray, 46, of Burbank, Calif. "If that's all she sees—women being brutalized, put down, oppressed, depressed, suppressed—after a while, she's going to grow up thinking, 'Well, that's the way I'm supposed to be treated.'"

But you cannot shelter your children from gangsta rap, counters Cameron Hughes, 33, of Youngstown, Ohio. How can his kids avoid the music and its relevancy, he asks, when they "watch kids get shot down in front of them. I don't have the luxury of censoring them. They're just telling it like it happens."

The current flak is no different from the controversy that surrounded some of the music the dads grew up with. "We must not forget we listened to Sly Stone, Jimi Hendrix and Janis Joplin," Sir Clark, 43, writes from South Central L.A. "There's no difference today between kids listening to music we don't like and when we listened to music our parents didn't like."

Rap is getting a bad rap, says Tony Camm, 33, Lynchburg, Va. "It's not the whole genre. Some rap is really good, like Queen Latifah."

—James T. Jones IV

Meanwhile, many Americans were calling for laws to control rap lyrics. These people objected to graphic sexual lyrics and songs in which fed-up characters take the law into their own hands. Opponents said such songs provoked racial conflict and violence in U.S. cities.

Latifah denounced the sexism and violence in some rap lyrics. But she agreed with the groups' social and political messages. She also supported the rappers' legal right to express opinions in their lyrics. The First Amendment of the U.S. Constitution grants Americans the right to speak, write, and publish anything they like, without fear of punishment. "A lot of what these guys are saying needs to be heard," she said. "They're bringing reality—the reality of the black culture—to a lot of people, pointing out things and exposing things that might be ignored otherwise."

Latifah sometimes used profanity in her lyrics. But she said her swearing was different from that of most male rappers. "It's the way the word is used," she explained. "When it's used to downgrade or denigrate you, that's when I have a problem with it."

Latifah felt that her message was equally important and also needed to be heard, especially by young black women. Her songs encouraged women to be independent and act with dignity. Her rapping was a way to share the lessons she'd learned from her mother.

Singles Success

Tommy Boy Records gave Latifah money to outfit herself for promotional photos. She used it to cement her image as a strong, self-respecting black woman. She went to an African clothing store in

Powerful: In this promotional photo for Tommy Boy Records, Queen Latifah stands strong. She expressed her hope for strength and unity within black communities through her music and appearance.

Newark and asked the owner to design a regal-looking outfit. She also bought accessories, including a crownlike hat. Unable to find shoes she liked, she posed barefoot for her first publicity photos. "People went crazy when they saw me," she said. "I was breaking the mold."

In 1988 Tommy Boy Records released "Wrath of My Madness" as a single. Lynch and Latifah were encouraged when it sold forty thousand copies. Latifah worked steadily on her music throughout that year. Soon she released two more singles, "Dance for Me" and "Ladies First."

On "Ladies First," Latifah collaborated with British rapper Monie Love (Simone Wilson). Its lyrics encourage women to take the lead in their lives. "Ladies First" became Latifah's first hit on the rhythm and blues (R & B) charts. The Rock and Roll Hall of Fame eventually named it one of "500 Songs That Shaped Rock and Roll."

As her music career became more demanding, Latifah made the difficult decision to leave college. She promised herself that she'd return to complete her degree someday. She also made another major life change. She moved out of the apartment she shared with her mother and brother and found her own place.

All Hail the Queen

In 1989 Tommy Boy Records released Queen Latifah's first full-length album, *All Hail the Queen*. Fans and critics loved it. One critic warned other rappers, "Male rappers step off, because the queen has arrived." Her debut album eventually sold more than one million copies and climbed to number six on the R & B chart.

All Hail the Queen was different from most rap albums. Like other rappers, Latifah used her music to voice opinions on a variety of social issues and to promote black pride. But unlike most other rappers, Latifah wrote from a woman's point of view. In songs like "Latifah's Law" and "Mama Gave Birth to the Soul Children," she explored the lives of young black women. Latifah's music appealed to a broad audience, including pop and alternative rock fans, because she rapped to a variety of background sounds, including reggae and jazz. She also departed from tradition by both rapping and singing on her album.

Latifah was not alone in her Afrocentricity, though. By 1989 Afrocentrism had become a popular cultural movement across the United States. Many black Americans had adopted African ways and were studying African history. Many black musicians, such as the rappers X-Clan, the Jungle Brothers, and Public Enemy, incorporated

Origins: The Jungle Brothers perform in 1991. This rap group included Afrocentric themes onstage.

The word *Afrocentric* first appeared in 1976. Molefi Kete Asante, a professor at Temple University in Philadelphia, Pennsylvania, introduced the concept. Asante supported the study of African history and culture from a non-European perspective.

Afrocentric themes into their music and stage presence. Some of these musicians wore clothes made from traditional African kente cloth.

"Afrocentricity is about being into yourself and into your people and being proud of your origins," Latifah said. "I was lucky to grow up in a very cultured family, and so Afrocentricity is something I've known all my life."

To promote *All Hail the Queen*, Latifah toured the United States and Europe. When she was onstage, she made sure her fans not only heard but also saw her message of dignity and self-respect. She rarely performed without a "crown." She expanded her wardrobe of regal, African-style clothes. She refused to wear revealing outfits. She expected the same from

On tour: Queen Latifah performs in 1990. She wore modest clothes and rarely performed without a "crown."

those who performed alongside her. "Sex sells, that's common sense," she said. "A lot of women sell their bodies. . . . That's not what I feel I need to do to sell a record. I'm not willing to sacrifice who I am."

Latifah also tried to foster racial tolerance and unity with her music. Critics praised her for expanding the boundaries of rap. Her unique style appealed to fans of different races, breaking barriers and busting stereotypes.

Taking Care of Business

Latifah enjoyed touring and performing, but she quickly realized that she lacked business skills. "My music career was careening ahead of my business savvy," she said. She had no road manager to collect payments after her shows. She had trouble dealing with concert promoters, who sometimes tried to shortchange her.

The historically white-controlled U.S. music industry has often exploited black performers. For example, in the early days of rock and roll, some white record producers used the material of black songwriters and performers without paying them. Whites used misleading contracts and false financial statements to steal money and recognition from black performers.

After a concert in Connecticut, a stubborn promoter wouldn't pay Latifah the fee they'd agreed upon. Latifah's friend Shakim was at the concert that night. He offered to collect the payment. "I don't know what he said to this promoter, but he returned in ten minutes with every penny I was owed," Latifah remembered. "I was not surprised.

Shakim knew how to take care of business."

Latifah saw that she needed help nurturing her career. She turned to the people she trusted the most. Shakim quit his job and became Latifah's business manager. Rita, still teaching at Irvington, managed her daughter's day-to-day business tasks while Latifah and Shakim were on the road. "Shakim and I and my mom learned the business together," Latifah explained.

Collaboration, Not Competition

Latifah's popularity grew when MTV broadcast her first music videos to international audiences. The "Ladies First" video got a lot of attention.

In this video, Latifah and Monie Love rap alongside photographs of influential black women and film clips of black protests in South Africa. Latifah is dressed in a uniform and walks around a giant map of southern Africa, replacing statuettes of military men (symbols of white power) with sculptures of raised fists (symbols of black pride and self-determination).

The video was not only a protest against apartheid but also a tribute to black women who have worked for justice in South Africa, the United States, and other countries where blacks have suffered discrimination. "I wanted to show the strength of black women in history," Latifah said. "I wanted to show what we've done. Sisters have been in the midst of things for a long time, but we just don't get to see it that much."

By collaborating with her rivals, Latifah avoided the rap industry's cutthroat competition. Male rappers were notorious for the boasting and insults in their lyrics. Female rappers one-upped their rivals too. But Latifah rarely glorified herself. When she did, her approach was witty instead of insulting.

"There's room for everybody," Latifah once said. "I don't feel threatened when other girls put out good records—I feel motivated to make a good record as well."

Drama Queen

As Latifah became better known, movie producers approached her with acting opportunities. Latifah jumped at the chance to make movies. She accepted a role in Spike Lee's urban drama *Jungle Fever*. "I love acting because I get to do things I might not do in real life," Latifah said. "It's fun, but a lot of hard work. When you see the finished deal, though, you know it was worth the energy and effort."

When *Jungle Fever* hit movie theaters in 1991, Latifah impressed audiences and critics. She played a waitress at a restaurant in Harlem, a black neighborhood in New York City, who gets angry when a married black customer brings his white girlfriend there. Latifah delivered her lines with a feisty, confident, no-nonsense attitude. Her screen time was brief. But it showed clearly that Latifah had the potential to be a good actor.

USA TODAY
A GANNETT COMPANY

CHAPTER SIX

Celebrity: Queen Latifah gets ready to play ball against basketball star Chris Mullen in 1992 during MTV's *Rock N' Jock Basketball*. The show pitted famous athletes against music stars.

Living Large

In the early 1990s, Queen Latifah was showered with awards, applause, and opportunities. In 1990 the readers of *Rolling Stone* magazine voted her Best Female Rapper. The largest music industry convention in the United States, the New Music Seminar in New York City, named her Best New Artist of 1990. Critics continued to praise her music and to recognize her potential beyond the rap world. They also credited her with raising the respectability of rap music.

Established music stars took note of the rising Queen too. Male rappers asked her to appear in their videos, hoping her presence would win female fans. When rocker David Bowie remade "Fame," a hit song of his from the 1970s, he invited Latifah to collaborate.

Her music even found its way into university classrooms. Within a year of *All Hail the Queen*'s release, students at Harvard University were studying Latifah's music. They discussed the cultural impact of her lyrics and her commitment to creating positive images in rap. Latifah felt honored when Harvard invited her to speak there. "It's a great feeling to know that people listen to you, that what you say makes a difference to them," she said.

Television Debut

After securing footholds in the music and movie industries, Latifah turned to television. In 1990 the American Broadcasting Company (ABC) invited Latifah to make her TV debut on a network Earth Day special. This two-hour program celebrated the twentieth anniversary of Earth Day. It featured some of the biggest names in U.S. music, cinema, television, and sports.

Soon Latifah was making regular television appearances on talk shows, variety shows, and sitcoms, including *In Living Color*, *Roc*, and *Hangin' with Mr. Cooper*. She also appeared in public service announcements for nonprofit organizations, such as Rock the Vote.

Rapper and actor Will Smith asked Latifah to make guest appearances on his popular TV program, *The Fresh Prince of Bel-Air*. This show was one of the most successful African American–themed TV programs of all time. Many people believe Smith paved the way for other rappers—including Latifah—to succeed in prime-time series television.

Latifah was determined to pursue an acting career on both the small screen and the big screen. She quickly accepted roles in *House Party 2* (1991) and *Juice* (1992), movies about urban African American youth.

TV time: Queen Latifah *(bottom, second from right)* makes a guest appearance in 1991 as Dee Dee on the TV show *The Fresh Prince of Bel-Air.*

Flavor Unit Management

As Latifah's career took off, she watched her fellow Flavor Unit members struggling to launch their careers. They too kept running into crooked club managers, concert promoters, and record company staff. "Many of us were so uneducated in business matters that [we were] constantly getting duped while filling the pockets of record companies," she said.

Anxious to help, Latifah and Shakim transformed their circle of friends into a formal business. They named it Flavor Unit Management. They established headquarters in Jersey City, New Jersey, which lies between Newark and New York City.

Flavor Unit Management began by managing the rap trio Naughty By Nature. As Naughty By Nature took off, other groups flocked to Flavor Unit. The company eventually grew into a successful management business representing scores of artists, including Apache, LL Cool J, Outkast, Next, and Monifah.

Flavor Unit Management gave Latifah a base from which to oversee her growing career. "I wanted to control my own destiny," Latifah said. Flavor Unit Management offered her the chance to do that.

Nature of a Sista

Latifah's expanding career did not keep her from her music. She worked hard to please her rap fans, releasing *Nature of a Sista* in late 1991.

Like *All Hail the Queen*, Latifah's second album broke down barriers between rap and mainstream music. "I've become more creative with melodies and things like that," she said at the time. "I am singing more and this album is really rhythmic." A reviewer described Latifah's work on this album as "singing from the heart with the influence of her mind."

But her lyrics remained classic Queen Latifah. She tackled tough issues, such as violence and teen pregnancy. She continued to promote self-respect, hard work, and black pride. In her song "Nuff of the Ruff Stuff," Latifah praised the power of self-confidence and optimism. In "One Mo' Time," she asked young black women to respect themselves and take responsibility for their lives. In "Fly Girl," she reminded men to respect women. "Bad as a Mutha" scolded girls and women for being materialistic, dating men only for their money. "There are a lot of girls out there who do that, and that's what I'm trying to change," Latifah explained.

She promoted *Nature of a Sista* by joining reggae artist Ziggy Marley on a national tour, performing nearly three hundred shows in one year. By this time, Latifah had abandoned her regal attire. She was afraid that fans were more interested in the royal theme than in her music.

"I stopped wearing the crowns . . . because people seemed to get too caught up in that," she said. "I'm more than just a hat."

Adjusting to Stardom

As soon as she was financially able, Latifah began to invest in her community. Doing so kept her rooted in reality. "Giving back is [a] great way to change up the way you see things," she said. Latifah gave back to East Orange by purchasing businesses and providing jobs for inner-city residents.

At the young age of twenty-one, Latifah was already living large. She was experiencing the success that she and her posse had fantasized about in Mark's basement. Her life was a whirl of recording sessions, concert dates, promotional events, movie sets, fan letters, and public appearances. Reporters, fans, critics, journalists, and politicians were talking about her in ways that she'd never even imagined.

Latifah's success did not surprise her mother. "I always knew my Dana was extraordinary," Rita said.

Latifah's rise to stardom did not, however, protect her from the problems many black Americans face. Most of the world, looking from a distance, saw Queen Latifah as a role model. Meanwhile, authorities who saw her up close often viewed her with suspicion.

Latifah described being stopped by police officers who wanted to know why a young black woman was driving an expensive BMW. She replied, "What do you mean what am I doing with this car? I earned this car. I paid for it in cash, in full." She later lamented, "I can't tell you how many times I've been stopped." Incidents like these frustrated and saddened Latifah. They reflected the social problems she addressed in her music.

Impression: Even though Queen Latifah was a role model and could afford nice things, she still was treated unfairly by some police because she was African American.

USA TODAY
Life
SECTION D
LIFE.USATODAY.COM

December 11, 1991

Queen Latifah, holding court

From the Pages of
USA TODAY

EAST ORANGE, N.J.—Her highness of hip-hop has hit the office, ready to rule. Queen Latifah perches behind the desk at her production firm, Flavor Unit Management, signing checks and issuing orders. At 21, Latifah is barely old enough to drink, but here, she's Head Rapper in Charge. "Every decision is mine as far as what I do and where I go."

Right now, she's doing plenty. Not only one of the top women in rap, she's also a promising businesswoman, producer and actress.

Her mother, Rita Owens, is the reason, Latifah says, she's matured so quickly. Divorced when Latifah was 9, Owens raised Latifah and her brother alone. The three now live separately, but Owens stays active in Latifah's life. When she's not teaching high school, Owens helps run Flavor Unit. She's the reason Latifah keeps her raps clean. "My mother is going to hear these records."

Latifah rarely talks about her father, a policeman, but credits him with teaching her "street smarts." That's how she survived puberty when she hung out in "four boroughs of New York."

She found distractions in school. "If I wasn't in school, I was playing basketball, or in somebody's basement, rhyming. "I used to hang out with these guys. We all rhymed. We all wanted to drive the Benz and have the real fat house on the hill. Rap was the way to do it for us."

She's just purchased a Jeep, a BMW and a house. But she won't be there much. She spends up to 300 days a year on the road. "When I'm home, people won't let me rest. Do this, do that. On tour, I've got to perform; that's all I have to do. That's when I'm having my fun. Rocking the house."

—James T. Jones IV

In honor: Queen Latifah performs in the summer of 1993 in California wearing her beloved brother Winki's motorcycle key around her neck.

Loving, Losing, Living

Winki Owens, like his famous sister, had found happiness and success. After high school, he stayed in New Jersey to be close to his family. Following in his father's footsteps, he trained at the police academy and joined the Newark police force.

Winki and Latifah led independent lives, but their bond remained strong. They found it hard to be apart. Latifah was so busy with writing, recording, and performing that she sometimes didn't see her brother for weeks.

Sibling bond: Queen Latifah *(above)* loved to spend time with her brother, Winki. They often rode motorcycles together.

When Winki and Latifah did get together, they liked to hop on their motorcycles and ride for miles. "When we were on the road together, we had a free, wild feeling that nothing else gave us . . . ," Latifah said. "It was our private realm. . . . Out there there, no one could bother us. We were one."

Family Plans

The time Latifah did spend with her family reminded her of how much she needed Winki and Rita. She wanted to make it easier for her family to spend time together. And she wanted to repay her mother and brother for all their support.

Latifah began hunting for a home to share with Rita and Winki. She sought a place that would give them each plenty of private space but would still allow the family togetherness they all wanted and needed. In nearby Wayne, New Jersey, she found a big unfinished house that she could design herself. Once she secured a home loan, Latifah began sketching the spaces she wanted.

Meanwhile, she was planning to develop affordable housing in northern New Jersey. She wanted to help low-income residents in her community who were trying to improve their lives. "Everybody on welfare is not trying to rip off the system," she said. "Some are using it as a stepping stone. . . . I want to provide the next step for them." She also wanted to ensure that lenders treated buyers with respect.

As she watched her house take shape, Latifah imagined all the

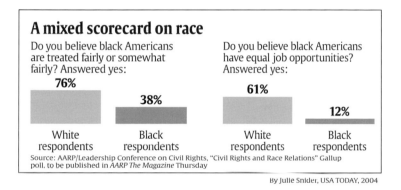

When Latifah applied for a mortgage (home loan), she faced the same problem Rita had. Despite her celebrity and wealth, "Queen Latifah could not get a mortgage," she said incredulously. "I had to go through three different companies. If I had to go through this, I can imagine what everybody else has to go through."

A mixed scorecard on race

Do you believe black Americans are treated fairly or somewhat fairly? Answered yes:

White respondents	Black respondents
76%	38%

Do you believe black Americans have equal job opportunities? Answered yes:

White respondents	Black respondents
61%	12%

Source: AARP/Leadership Conference on Civil Rights, "Civil Rights and Race Relations" Gallup poll, to be published in *AARP The Magazine* Thursday

By Julie Snider, USA TODAY, 2004

good times she'd share with Winki and Rita in the years ahead. But a few weeks before the house was finished, a tragedy shattered Latifah's plan to reunite her family.

Shattered Dreams

Latifah, Rita, and Shakim had recently given Winki a new motorcycle for his twenty-fourth birthday. It was a fast and powerful Kawasaki Ninja. In April 1992, Winki was riding his motorcycle around East Orange. A car hit him, and he and his bike went under the car.

Latifah and Shakim were helping their friend Latee move a couch into his new apartment. Ramsey called with the news about Winki. Too shaken to drive, Latifah asked Shakim to take her to the hospital.

As they drove, a chill spread through her body. Latifah knew instinctively that her brother's condition was grim.

When Shakim and Latifah arrived at the hospital, her fears were confirmed. Winki's friends looked at her without a word. Rita sat with tears in her eyes but, otherwise, eerily calm. Everybody waited in excruciating silence. Finally, a doctor entered the room. She said, "I'm sorry. He's gone."

Latifah screamed at the doctor, ordering her to go back and help Winki. She refused to believe he was dead.

The months following Winki's death were the lowest point of Latifah's life. "I loved him so much that I didn't want to live," she remembered. "If I couldn't share my life, my successes . . . my dreams, and my thoughts with him, it wasn't worth it." To make matters worse, she blamed herself. "I never imagined that bike, bought in love, would be the cause of Winki's death," she said.

Normally strong and disciplined, Latifah couldn't cope with the overwhelming pain of losing Winki. She looked for ways to numb her pain. She woke up crying. She walked around in a daze and wore sunglasses to hide her tears. She played basketball most of the day, taking out her anger on the court. When she became exhausted, she drank alcohol and smoked marijuana to shut out her feelings until she fell asleep.

Latifah had trouble concentrating on her work. "When Winki died, the song in me died," she said.

Black Reign

Despite the tragedy, Latifah had obligations to fulfill. She had signed a contract with Motown Records. She examined her options. "I could choose to wallow in my pain and grief, or I could choose to get up and get through it," she said. "I made a choice to live."

After making that choice, Latifah had to find new ways to get through the day. At first she spent long days at Winki's grave, talking to him. It brought her peace.

Then she forced herself to face her motorcycle. It reminded her of Winki, and she felt that riding without him would betray their bond. "But my brother's spirit was asking me to ride, and live, for his sake . . . ," she recalled. So she got back on the bike. "When I'm on that bike, I'm talking to Winki. And I'm talking to God. I'm saying, 'Okay, Lord, take care of me now.'"

Once Latifah had made her peace with Winki, with her motorcycle, and with God, her strength and focus slowly returned. She realized that to keep healing, she needed to make music. So she headed back into the studio. She began working on her third album, *Black Reign.* She poured her complicated feelings into her songs.

In the song "Winki's Theme," she paid tribute to her big brother. "It was a message of pure love for my brother," she explained.

Reflecting on the making of *Black Reign*, Latifah recalled, "Mom later said the album title perfectly summed up my life in that moment: It was a black period, but one over which I would ultimately reign. The queen inside me was alive again."

Moving Forward

Latifah worked hard to move forward in her personal life. Meanwhile, her professional life was soaring.

She released *Black Reign* in late 1993. Latifah continued to rap on this album. But she also did more traditional singing than on her first two albums. The musical range of *Black Reign*—from rap to R & B to jazz—demonstrated Latifah's immense talent. The album was a hot seller. It became the first gold album (the first album to sell five hundred thousand copies) by a solo female rap artist.

After *Black Reign*, Latifah shifted her creative energies to focus on acting. She landed her first major dramatic role in the 1993 movie *My*

Latifah dedicated *Black Reign* to Winki. For the CD's back cover, she chose a photo of herself sitting next to her brother's grave.

Life. The movie stars Michael Keaton as Bob Jones, a man with terminal cancer who makes a video autobiography for the child he and his wife are expecting. Critics praised Latifah for her performance as Theresa, the nurse who cares for Bob toward the end of his life.

Living Single

Latifah's versatility as an actor impressed executives at Fox television network. They offered her a lead role in *Living Single*, a new situation comedy (sitcom) about young black professional women in New York City. Fox producer Yvette Lee Bowser created the show. She hoped to provide intelligent, successful female role models for African American viewers.

Like Latifah's music, *Living Single* cast black women in a positive light rather than using negative stereotypes. She accepted the role and both wrote and sang the show's theme song. The first episode aired in August 1993.

Bright women: Queen Latifah *(center left)* acts with her costars, from left, Erika Alexander, Kim Fields, and Kim Coles, in the hit TV show *Living Single*, which first aired in 1993. The ladies were role models for African American women.

October 8, 1993

Queen Latifah's latest domain

From the Pages of
USA TODAY

BURBANK, Calif.—Being one of rap's top female stars at age 23 wasn't enough for Queen Latifah. She was ready to take on television, too. So when she heard that Fox wanted to do a sitcom about four upwardly mobile black women, she jumped. "I thought it would be a nice way to introduce myself to the country, as opposed to just music fans," says Latifah.

She made a good move. *Living Single* is shaping up as a solid hit for Fox.

Doing a sitcom is a far cry from rapping for Latifah; she's now working days instead of nights, spending most of her time rehearsing and memorizing lines. "I'm not a morning person," she says. "In music, everything happens at night. This is a 9 to 5 job."

She's happy to be working with *Living Single* creator and co-executive producer Yvette Denise Lee [Yvette Lee Bowser], who is black. "I felt that she could write from our point of view," Latifah says. "

Latifah's concern about her role—Khadijah, the tough editor of *Flavor* magazine—was that she be down to earth. "That's who I am," she says. "People respect me for what I'm doing, and I didn't want to do anything to jeopardize my integrity."

Latifah hasn't turned her back on her recording career. A new album, *Black Reign*, will be in stores Nov. 16, released on her own record label, Flavor Unit Records, which is distributed by Motown.

She also is chief executive officer of a management firm whose clients include Naughty By Nature, FU-Schnickens, Apache and Nikki D. She's been flying back to New Jersey on weekends to tend to business.

Now that she's conquered TV, she hopes to one day run a magazine like her TV alter ego. "I'll do everything by the time I'm 30," she says.

—Jefferson Graham

Living Single revolved around the lives of six friends: roommates Khadijah (Latifah), Synclaire (Kim Coles), and Regina (Kim Fields); their neighbors Overton (John Henton) and Kyle (T. C. Carson); and frequent visitor Maxine (Erika Alexander). A strong and determined entrepreneur, Khadijah is the publisher of *Flavor*, a magazine for women. She works hard to make it succeed. Khadijah surrounds herself with family and longtime friends. With sharp intelligence and a quick wit, she often acts as mediator and negotiator. She is the group's anchor.

Accepting a role on *Living Single* meant living in Los Angeles, California, during the production season. This grueling season ran from late summer through spring. Actors reported to the studio as early as six in the morning and might work fourteen to sixteen hours per day. Like other TV shows, *Living Single* took a break each summer. During these months, Latifah could pursue movie roles and spend time writing and recording music.

Flavor Unit Management had grown to ten full-time employees by 1994. Latifah was thousands of miles away, so Shakim took the reins. Latifah kept tabs on the company from afar. During filming breaks, she listened to demo tapes and reviewed the business reports that staff express-mailed to her each week.

Latifah was living a demanding life. But she made time for fun too. "You can't make it through all this without a social life," she said. She enjoyed checking out the Los Angeles nightclub scene. She learned kickboxing. And naturally, she rode her motorcycle whenever she could.

Accolades and Obstacles

Living Single was a huge hit. At the end of its first season (1993–1994), *Living Single* was Fox's best-rated new program. Soon it was the most watched show in African American households.

Latifah sometimes had trouble enjoying her popularity. "I'm on TV! I should be like YAAAHHHH!" she said, waving her hands excitedly. "But it doesn't mean what it should mean. And that's because I'm not feeling all the way. I wish my brother were here . . . just to experience some of this with me."

The year 1995 started on a high note for Latifah. She won two major awards in March. At the Soul Train Music Awards, she received the Sammy Davis Jr. Award for Entertainer of the Year. And at the Grammy Awards, her song "U.N.I.T.Y." from *Black Reign* won a Grammy for Best Rap Solo Performance. Latifah had written the song after witnessing abusive behavior between men and women at a picnic in Philadelphia. The song is a salute to women. It also reminds listeners that disrespect, insults, and physical abuse work against unity among black people.

Winner: Queen Latifah shows off her Sammy Davis Jr. Award for Entertainer of the Year at the Soul Train Music Awards in 1995.

Later that year, the very violence Latifah criticized in her music overshadowed her successes. In July 1995, while she was driving with friends in Harlem, two youths carjacked her BMW. They shot one of her friends, Sean Moon, in the stomach and the chest.

Without stopping to think, Latifah stepped into traffic and flagged down a passing car for a ride to the hospital. Medical staff praised Latifah's quick thinking. "If Moon's treatment had been delayed by 15 minutes, 'he would have bled out,' said his surgeon."

Police quickly caught the carjackers. They were later tried and jailed. But the incident changed Latifah's confident attitude and care-free lifestyle. Afraid for her safety, she hired more bodyguards. For a while, she rarely went out socially. "I'm looking over my shoulder all the time," she said. She also carried a gun.

USA TODAY
Life
SECTION D
LIFE.USATODAY.COM

April 25, 1996

Tearful Queen Latifah recounts carjacking

From the Pages of USA TODAY

A weepy Queen Latifah, 26, testified Wednesday at the New York trial of Ricardo Rodriguez, 19, one of two men accused of carjacking the rapper and shooting her friend.

Latifah said the July incident left her feeling unsafe and resulted in her pleading guilty last month in Los Angeles to carrying a gun in her car.

While Rodriguez hopped in the front seat of her $67,000 1995 BMW, Rashien Fortune, 19, shot Sean Moon, who, along with Lynn Mayo, was celebrating a reunion with Latifah, police allege. Moon survived.

Latifah testified she "heard Lynn saying, 'He's hit! He's hit! Sean's hit!' I said, 'Sean, are you hit?' ... He lifted his shirt, and blood was coming from his side."

A passer-by offered to drive the trio to a nearby hospital. The rapper said that in the car, she reassured Moon when he told her, "I'm going to die."

Trial: Queen Latifah *(front)* answers questions from the media beside her friend Lynn Mayo, who also witnessed the carjacking.

Rodriguez, who offered to plead guilty three times, opted for a trial after being told he would receive the same 7-to-21-year sentence as his accomplice. "The numbers are too high," he told his trial judge.

—USA TODAY reporters

A few months after the attack, police stopped Latifah for speeding in Los Angeles. When they searched her car, they found a loaded pistol and marijuana. They arrested her. Later, a judge found her guilty of carrying a loaded and concealed firearm and of possessing drugs. The judge fined Latifah, gave her two years' probation, and required her to make a donation to a Los Angeles charity.

The negative news coverage was difficult for Latifah to swallow. She knew she was a role model for thousands of young people. She worked hard to let kids know that she'd made a mistake.

Set It Off

Latifah's portrayal of down-to-earth Khadijah gained her even more

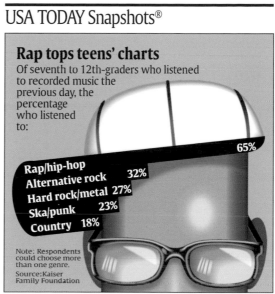

USA TODAY Snapshots®

Rap tops teens' charts

Of seventh to 12th-graders who listened to recorded music the previous day, the percentage who listened to:

65%

Rap/hip-hop

Alternative rock 32%

Hard rock/metal 27%

Ska/punk 23%

Country 18%

Note: Respondents could choose more than one genre.
Source: Kaiser Family Foundation

By Rebecca Pollack and Bob Laird, USA TODAY, 2006

fans. Movie producers continued to approach her with acting roles. Latifah found herself choosing from many offers, and she made her decisions carefully.

"First, I read the script and decide if I like my place in the film," she said. "I read the role to see if it is meaty, to see if it is something I can get into, something I feel I am capable of doing, something challenging. Then I look at who is involved with it, directing it and starring in it. I look at the package, the chemistry and the track record of whoever is involved."

Latifah surprised her fans by accepting a role in the violent film

True acting: Queen Latifah *(center right)* starred in *Set It Off* with *(from left)* Jada Pinkett, Kimberly Elise, and Vivica Fox in 1996. Latifah won the Best Actress award from the Acapulco Black Film Festival for her role in this film.

Set It Off (1996). In this movie, four young black women try to escape their dead-end lives in a Los Angeles ghetto by robbing banks. Friends since childhood, the four characters struggle with low-paying jobs, sexism, racism, and grief. One character loses her younger brother when police kill him in a case of mistaken identity. Another character must give up her toddler son when a social worker decides she is an unfit mother. Another loses her job just because she happens to know someone who committed a crime. Latifah played the role of Cleo, a tough lesbian who drinks too much and takes drugs. Cleo is an unrepentant outlaw—and mother hen to the other three women.

Latifah took this role because she believed the film delivered an important message about the lives of black Americans. It portrayed the hopelessness and violence that Latifah witnessed in Hyatt Court and East Orange. She also relished the acting challenge. "That's the first real acting role I've gotten as far as I'm concerned," she said. "It was so not me that I had to work hard on becoming that person and proving that I could do it, that I could act."

Latifah's performance received high praise from film critics. Stephen Holden of the *New York Times* wrote, "In a performance of explosive emotional heat, the popular rap star makes this potentially unsympathetic character the most endearing of the four." In 1997 the Acapulco Black Film Festival gave her its Best Actress award for her work in *Set It Off*.

Flavor Unit West

As Latifah's acting career flourished, so did her management company. Flavor Unit Management had launched a record label, Flavor Unit Records, in 1995. Since then Latifah and Shakim had expanded from managing artists to recording them.

In 1996 Flavor Unit opened a West Coast office to represent R & B artist Monica and other singers based in California. Having a California office also helped Latifah develop her growing TV and film career. Latifah asked her old friend Ramsey Gbelawoe to head the California operation as general manager.

By 1997 Flavor Unit Management was representing ten groups. "It's incredible to look back over the years and see how far we've come," said Latifah. "I've always believed that

Represent: Monica performs in 1998. Queen Latifah's company, Flavor Unit Management, represented this popular performer.

someone who's moving up should always take the time to look back and give a hand to the next young person trying to make some moves."

Endings and Beginnings

Living Single continued to be a hit with viewers. And in 1996, the National Association for the Advancement of Colored People (NAACP) had given the show its Image Award for Outstanding Comedy Series. Nonetheless, Fox executives canceled the show at the end of the 1996–1997 season.

Thousands of shocked fans across the country wrote letters protesting the cancellation. The network brought back the show for another season.

Living Single was canceled for good after the 1997–1998 season. The year it ended, the show received a second NAACP Image Award for Outstanding Comedy Series.

"I was sad that I was losing the daily camaraderie of my friends; hanging out every day and doing something fun, making people laugh and giving the fans a show they enjoyed," Latifah said soon after the show was canceled. "But I also was excited about . . . being free to do more things in terms of film, to have that time available and that mobility," she added. "There's always going to be life after *Living Single*."

Range: Queen Latifah portrayed a jazz singer in the film *Living Out Loud* in 1998. Her smooth, sultry voice surprised fans who knew her only as a rap star.

Evolving Persona

Life after *Living Single* was as busy and exciting as Latifah had hoped it would be. While wrapping up the sitcom, she tackled a variety of other acting roles, demonstrating her impressive range. In the science fiction thriller film *Sphere* (1998), Latifah played a deep-sea diver who helps scientists examine a mysterious glowing sphere on the seafloor. The TV miniseries *Mama Flora's Family* (1998) featured Latifah as the angry and frustrated granddaughter of a family matriarch.

In the movie *Living Out Loud* (1998), Latifah played the role of a jazz singer alongside costars Holly Hunter and Danny DeVito. She described this performance as "the best work I've done since *Set It Off.*" Fans and critics agreed. They were stunned when Latifah filled movie theaters with a sultry voice so unlike her rap style. One reviewer wrote, "As good as Hunter and DeVito are, it's all they can do to keep the movie from being stolen out from under them when Queen Latifah is onscreen. . . . Latifah binds the audience to her as easily and gracefully as she assays the notes."Her performance in *Living Out Loud* created an instant following among jazz lovers. Other viewers begged Latifah to record a jazz album and declared their new respect for the queen of rap.

Order in the Court

Latifah's busy acting schedule had slowed down her music making. But she hadn't forgotten about hip-hop. As soon as *Living Single* went off

Back to music: Queen Latifah released her fourth album, *Order in the Court*, in 1998.

the air, Latifah released her fourth album, *Order in the Court*. Motown and Flavor Unit Records coproduced this album. "I was excited . . . to get back involved and become more hands-on with my company and put my album out and be able to go on the road and push it," she said.

Order in the Court reflected an older, more contemplative Latifah. On this album, she mused aloud about life and death, social problems, and various ideas and events that were on her mind. Her song "What Ya Gonna Do" expressed the sadness she still felt about Winki's death. "Life" was a tribute to the rappers Tupac Shakur and the Notorious B.I.G., who had died in separate shooting incidents in 1996 and 1997. In "Black on Black Love," Latifah hailed the importance of caring for one another.

"It's where I am at this point in my life," Latifah said of *Order in the Court.* "Thinking about love, thinking about lust. Thinking 'bout life, thinking about God, thinking about nothing but beats and rhymes. There is a song that reflects each one of those kind of thoughts or emotions."

Self-Portrait

After releasing *Order in the Court,* Latifah decided that she wanted to reach even more women with her message of self-respect. Collaborating with *New York Daily News* reporter Karen Hunter, Latifah wrote her autobiography. "I'm writing this book to let every woman know that she, too—no matter what her status or her place in life—is royalty," she explained.

In January 1999, publisher William Morrow and Company released *Ladies First: Revelations of a Strong Woman.* In it Latifah shared her positive attributes and

Writer: Queen Latifah promotes her book *Ladies First* at a book signing in New York City in 1999.

accomplishments with readers. She also wrote about not-so-proud moments in her life, such as lying to her parents as a child, using drugs, and getting arrested.

Critics applauded Latifah for her honest self-portrait. One critic wrote, "The successful actress and rap singer offers a frank, down-to-earth . . . review of the hard life lessons she has learned, about self-respect, love, and independence. . . . Latifah delivers her insights with a biographical frankness . . . and salty directness that her young female fans . . . are likely to find engaging and convincing." By July 1999, Latifah's life story had reached the number four spot on the Blackboard African-American Bestsellers nonfiction list.

A New Challenge

As a new century approached, Latifah continued to work hard on her career. As a writer for *Ebony* magazine noted, "She is not one to rest on her laurels or her butt."

Latifah had big projects in the works for her music, her company,

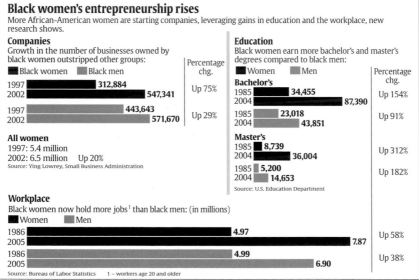

Black women's entrepreneurship rises

More African-American women are starting companies, leveraging gains in education and the workplace, new research shows.

Companies

Growth in the number of businesses owned by black women outstripped other groups:

■ Black women   ■ Black men

		Percentage chg.
1997	312,884	
2002	547,341	Up 75%
1997	443,643	
2002	571,670	Up 29%

All women

1997: 5.4 million
2002: 6.5 million   Up 20%
Source: Ying Lowrey, Small Business Administration

Education

Black women earn more bachelor's and master's degrees compared to black men:

■ Women   ■ Men

		Percentage chg.
Bachelor's		
1985	34,455	Up 154%
2004	87,390	
1985	23,018	Up 91%
2004	43,851	
Master's		
1985	8,739	Up 312%
2004	36,004	
1985	5,200	Up 182%
2004	14,653	

Source: U.S. Education Department

Workplace

Black women now hold more jobs[1] than black men: (in millions)

■ Women   ■ Men

		Percentage chg.
1986	4.97	Up 58%
2005	7.87	
1986	4.99	Up 38%
2005	6.90	

Source: Bureau of Labor Statistics   1 – workers age 20 and older

By Alejandro Gonzalez, USA TODAY, 2006

Action packed: Queen Latifah stars alongside Denzel Washington in the 1999 movie *The Bone Collector*. Latifah played the nurse of Washington's character.

and her acting. She was already working on a new album. She planned to have Flavor Unit Records record and distribute this album independently, so she could have complete control of it. Meanwhile, Flavor Unit Entertainment grew to include two more record labels, Jersey Kids and Ghetto Works. And in fall 1999, the thriller *The Bone Collector* hit movie theaters. Latifah played a nurse who cares for a paralyzed detective (Denzel Washington) obsessed with catching a serial killer.

At the same time, Latifah embarked on a brand-new adventure. Shakim had long encouraged her to do a talk show. Successful talkshow host Rosie O'Donnell had too. So Latifah rose to the challenge.

In September 1999, she launched *The Queen Latifah Show*. Latifah not only hosted the show, but she also coproduced it with Shakim. The show featured live music, celebrity guests, regular appearances by Latifah's mother, and solution-oriented discussions about social issues.

January 27, 1999

TV's chatfest expanding with Latifah

From the Pages of
USA TODAY

NEW ORLEANS—Queen Latifah is poised to enter the talk-show fray next fall. Her contrast to current hosts may give her a better shot at success.

Latifah expects to offer viewers a grab bag of material. She plans musical segments and guest stars some days, and serious discussion about women's issues at other times.

Latifah, 28, first considered a show amid rumors that Oprah Winfrey might step down. Oprah didn't, but Latifah wanted in anyway, after well-received movie roles (*Living Out Loud*) and a five-year TV run on Fox's *Living Single*.

"I come from a unique background, I'm down-to-earth, and people feel like they can talk to me," she says. "I'm young enough to draw a hip crowd, but at the same time I'm mature enough and classy enough to bring in older viewers."

As for role models, "we'll take a little bit from Oprah, a little bit from Rosie (O'Donnell) and a little bit from Chris Rock . . . but I don't think it'll be like any of those shows. It'll be like me."

—Gary Levin

As the show launched, Latifah explained, "I'm trying to capture an audience that I feel hasn't been spoken to. . . . It's going to be real, as real as I can keep it. And it's going to be positive."

Running a company, recording an album, looking for new film roles, and taping *The Queen Latifah Show* five days a week was an intense life. She often worked fourteen or more hours per day, and she managed two hardworking staffs—one at Flavor Unit and one

Her own show: Queen Latifah talks with U.S. vice president Al Gore in October 2000 on *The Queen Latifah Show*. The show aired five days a week.

for the talk show. "There are a lot of people who work real hard to make things happen," she said. "I'm respectful of what my employees do. . . . I'm not a mean boss."

When she found time to relax, she headed to the basketball court and enjoyed the company of good friends. She divided her time between New York City, where she aired her show, and her home in New Jersey.

A big role: Queen Latifah plays the part of prison matron Mama Morton in the movie *Chicago* (2002). The movie was a huge hit with audiences.

The Mother of Reinvention

The Queen Latifah Show lasted two seasons. It was canceled due to low ratings. Its final show aired on August 31, 2001.

Latifah was philosophical about the cancellation. She'd worked hard but knew she faced tough competition. "My talk show wasn't a raving success," she reflected. "If it was, I'd still be doing it. . . . I tried my best. But you can't beat Oprah at her game." She picked herself up, dusted herself off, and started on her next big adventure.

Movie Maven

Latifah's next project turned out to be a very big deal indeed. She landed the part of prison matron Mama Morton in the movie musical *Chicago* (2002). This movie tells the story of two female murderers competing for fame in an effort to avoid execution.

Chicago was a huge hit with fans and critics. It won six Academy Awards (Oscars) and several other awards as well. Its cast, crew, and creators were nominated for dozens of additional awards. Latifah received an Academy Award nomination for Best Supporting Actress.

Latifah was the first female rapper ever to earn an Oscar nomination. Even though she didn't win the award, she was ecstatic to be short-listed for it. Executive producer Craig Zadan recalled, "After the nominations, she was giggling and screaming."

Over the next decade, Latifah appeared onscreen many times. She played roles in more than two dozen movies, including Charlene Morton in the comedy film *Bringing Down the House* (2003), Aunt Em in the TV movie *The Muppets' Wizard of Oz* (2005), Ana Wallace

Oscar nod: Queen Latifah arrives at the 75th Annual Academy Awards in 2003. Latifah was nominated for Best Supporting Actress for her work in *Chicago*.

It took Latifah three auditions to convince *Chicago* director Rob Marshall that he should cast her as Mama Morton but convince him she did. She beat out several superstars—Kathy Bates, Bette Midler, Liza Minnelli, Rosie O'Donnell, and Whoopi Goldberg—to get the part.

in the TV movie *Life Support* (2007), Motormouth Maybelle in the movie musical *Hairspray* (2007), August Boatwright in the drama film *Secret Life of Bees* (2008), the voice of woolly mammoth Ellie in three sequels to the animated movie *Ice Age* (2006–2012), and Vi Rose Hill in the musical comedy *Joyful Noise* (2012).

In addition to acting in movies, Latifah also tried her hand at producing them. She specialized in comedies. Her producing credits included *Bringing Down the House, The*

Movie musical: Queen Latifah *(right)* plays the part of Motormouth Maybelle alongside John Travolta *(left)* in the movie *Hairspray* (2007).

In 2006 Queen Latifah became the first hip-hop artist to earn a star on the Hollywood Walk of Fame.

Cookout (2004), *Beauty Shop* (2005), *The Perfect Holiday* (2007), and *Just Wright* (2010). She acted in each of the movies she produced.

Latifah's acting and producing in the early twenty-first century produced a mixed bag of results. Some efforts, such as *Bringing Down the House*, were loved by fans but panned by reviewers. Others, such as *Hairspray* and *The Secret Life of Bees*, earned several awards and nominations as well as box-office success. And some films, such as *The Perfect Holiday*, were all-around flops.

Superstar: Queen Latifah flashes a peace sign while receiving her star on the Hollywood Walk of Fame in Los Angeles, California, in 2006.

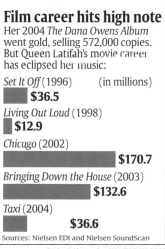

Film career hits high note

Her 2004 *The Dana Owens Album* went gold, selling 572,000 copies. But Queen Latifah's movie career has eclipsed her music:

Set It Off (1996)   (in millions)
$36.5

Living Out Loud (1998)
$12.9

Chicago (2002)
$170.7

Bringing Down the House (2003)
$132.6

Taxi (2004)
$36.6

Sources: Nielsen EDI and Nielsen SoundScan

By Joni Alexander, USA TODAY, 2005

Latifah accepted all these results with grace. "The movies I made weren't always huge box office or critical successes," she said. "Sure, I want them to earn millions . . . but it doesn't always work out that way. . . . I sleep at night knowing I did my best."

Jazz Journey

Latifah's rapping had opened the door to acting for her. And acting, in turn, sent Latifah on a new vocal journey. After her singing roles in *Living Out Loud* and *Chicago*, both Latifah and her fans wanted more. So she began recording an album of classic jazz, blues, and rock songs. "I felt like the timing was good to go ahead and do this," Latifah explained.

In 2004 she released *The Dana Owens Album* on the rock label Interscope Records. Giving background on the album's title, a reporter wrote, "She used her given name as a way of letting people know that before she was the rapper-turned-actress Queen Latifah, she was Dana Owens, a girl who loved to sing."

Indeed, the timing was right for *The Dana Owens Album*. It was obvious to listeners that Latifah had poured her soul into her singing. Critics agreed she'd made an impressive album. One reviewer wrote, "The recording . . . is a tribute to Ms. Owens's talents and her musical tastes, and an example of what the so-called hip-hop generation can produce, when we allow them to grow up." The album was nominated for the 2005 Grammy Award for Best Jazz Vocal Album.

Latifah had so much fun making *The Dana Owens Album* that she wanted to do another similar one. So she headed back into the studio. In 2007 she released *Trav'lin' Light*, this time on Verve Records, a leading jazz label.

Trav'lin' Light was equally well received. It reached number one on the jazz charts, number six on the R & B charts, and number eleven on the pop charts. One critic wrote, "*Trav'lin' Light*, Queen Latifah's follow-up to her first collection of pop standards . . . is, if anything,

Center stage: Queen Latifah hosts the 47th Annual Grammy Awards in Los Angeles, California, in 2005. That year *The Dana Owens Album* was nominated for Best Jazz Vocal Album.

even better than that Grammy-nominated set." *Trav'lin Light* went on to earn a Grammy nomination of its own for Best Traditional Pop Vocal Album in 2008.

By 2008 she had already finished recording her next album, *Persona*. On this album, Latifah returned to her hip-hop roots. She released *Persona* in 2009 on the Flavor Unit Records label.

Persona hit the market with a thud, selling considerably fewer copies than Latifah's earlier albums. Music critics, like music buyers, gave it a lukewarm reception.

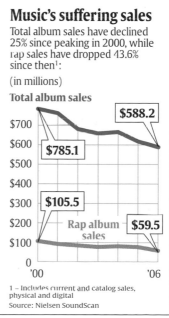

Music's suffering sales

Total album sales have declined 25% since peaking in 2000, while rap sales have dropped 43.6% since then[1]:

(in millions)

Total album sales

$785.1

$588.2

$700
$600
$500
$400
$300 — $105.5
$200 — Rap album sales — $59.5
$100
0
'00   '06

1 – Includes current and catalog sales, physical and digital
Source: Nielsen SoundScan

By Julie Snider, USA TODAY, 2007

Giving Back

Even when Latifah is cutting an album, filming a movie, running her company, or writing a book—or all of these at once—she still makes time to give back to her community. Shortly after Winki's death, she founded the Lancelot H. Owens Scholarship Foundation, a charitable division of Flavor Unit Entertainment.

The foundation provides money to send inner-city kids to college and provide other forms of academic support. This support includes professional mentors, academic and career counselors, internship placement services, and more. Latifah's friends and colleagues in the entertainment industry help the foundation raise funds.

"Kids are our future," Latifah explains. "I treasure the fact that when you give a child an education, you allow him or her the freedom to dream and to become an amazing person.... That person you helped to educate may come back and help another kid. It moves us all forward."

In addition to advocating for inner-city youths, Latifah is a strong supporter of groups that support sick and homeless children, groups that fight human trafficking, and athletic organizations for girls and women. "I've never regretted giving money away to someone who is less fortunate," she says. "I give it with freedom, knowing that what I am really doing is giving myself a gift."

When Latifah gives an interview, makes a public appearance, or writes a book, she encourages others to give back to their communities. "You don't even have to spend money to give," she points out. "Try to incorporate giving into your life as much as possible.... You never know what kind of impact you can have on [a] person's life with a small act of kindness."

Support: Queen Latifah speaks at the awards reception of the Lancelot H. Owens Scholarship Foundation in 2006. She founded this charity, which supports youth.

Reviewers called it "odd," "schizophrenic," "a bit of a mess," "a missed opportunity,"and "easily her least essential release."

But Latifah has never been one to dwell on disappointments. "I don't make a record expecting to go platinum," she said. "I make music because something inside me is aching to get out."

A Work in Progress

While Latifah took the movie and music world by storm, she also took the time to care for herself and others. First, she focused on her own body. Although she loved her shape and had never suffered from the self-loathing that plagues many women, she felt unwell. "I was at my heaviest when I was playing matron 'Mama' Morton in *Chicago*. . . . I wasn't feeling my best. I was sluggish. My back hurt. . . . I just wanted to feel better, be healthy, have more energy." So she began an exercise program. She also started eating healthier foods. And she has stayed committed to her health.

"Exercise has become inextricably linked with my self-esteem," she explained. She said that living a healthier life had become crucial to not only her physical but also her mental well-being. "We make our worst decisions when we're not feeling our best. . . . But we empower ourselves when we put our health and well-being first."

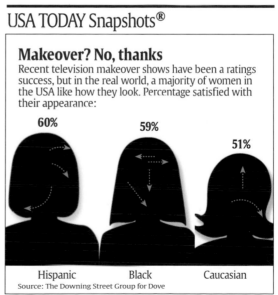

USA TODAY Snapshots®

Makeover? No, thanks

Recent television makeover shows have been a ratings success, but in the real world, a majority of women in the USA like how they look. Percentage satisfied with their appearance:

60% Hispanic
59% Black
51% Caucasian

Source: The Downing Street Group for Dove

By Charlotte E. Tucker and Julie Snider, USA TODAY, 2004

USA TODAY Life SECTION D
LIFE.USATODAY.COM

October 7, 2009

Queen Latifah: 'Persona' grata

From the Pages of
<u>USA TODAY</u>

NEW YORK—Stepping off the elevator at a posh Midtown hotel, Queen Latifah is approached by a fan who notes, with some surprise, that she has slimmed down.

Latifah smiles easily. "I needed to," says the rapper/singer/songwriter/actress/film producer/celebrity spokeswoman, who last year added the Jenny Craig diet line to her string of endorsement deals.

But the multitasking artist born Dana Owens isn't here to discuss her weight loss, or to promote anyone's product other than her own. Settling into a booth in the lobby, Latifah orders English Breakfast tea, with milk and sugar, and begins talking about her new album, *Persona*. It's her first collection of original, hip-hop-driven songs in more than a decade, following two albums on which she covered traditional pop, jazz and soul tunes.

Persona contributors include fellow notables such as Missy Elliott, Mary J. Blige, Busta Rhymes and the production team Cool & Dre. Results range from the driving single "Cue the Rain," which Latifah describes as "almost a rock record," to "My Couch," "where I'm imagining that my guy has had a hard day of work, and I'm going to make sure he has all the loving he wants when he gets home. There's a lot of love on this album."

Latifah, 39, is less forthcoming about her romantic life. "I never comment on that," she says, gently but firmly. But she does open up about the inspiration for "The World," an uncharacteristically hard-bitten track. In the song, Latifah alludes to having been molested as a 5-year-old child; her assailant was a male babysitter.

"It was important for me to write that, to get it off my chest," she says. "And to discuss it with a therapist, and tell my parents—which I did, eventually, though it took me about 20 years. And hopefully it will be helpful to someone out there who has gone through a similar situation."

The incident "left me not knowing how to deal with certain things. Boys can put pressure on you, and I didn't do so well with saying no. I had a lot to figure out, and

I did eventually, but it was tough. We have to do a better job of looking out for our young girls, because there are predators out there."

Latifah also expresses concern for her female peers. "Never in my career do I remember rap being so male-dominated. In videos, women are basically shown as the girl you shake the booty with. They're objectified. There are females out there who can rap, who listen to rap. Missy and Lil' Kim and the young up-and-coming ones need an opportunity to be heard. I think we're all masculine and feminine, and a society can't be right if you don't honor the feminine voice."

Such forthright positions are integral to Latifah's enduring appeal, says former *Vibe* editor Alan Light. "Hip-hop applauds succeeding on your own terms, and she's done that. She's always been true to the image she created: proud, strong, socially aware. Those qualities are there whether in her music, her movies or when she's hosting award shows."

Though Latifah likes to play film characters who share her strength, "they don't have to be that way," she says. "A good script is always the starting point." Having voiced the role of a pregnant mammoth for this summer's animated *Ice Age: Dawn of the Dinosaurs*, she'll turn up next year opposite fellow rapper/actor Common in the romantic comedy *Just Wright*.

Latifah also will kick off a month-long concert tour Nov. 1 in Seattle [Washington]. "I know I'll have so much fun rocking these new songs on stage, and, of course, playing older favorites." Covergirl, the tour's sponsor, has launched a video contest on QueenLatifah.com to choose opening acts in select cities. A grand-prize winner will score a record contract and the chance to be featured in a national print ad for Latifah's Covergirl Queen Collection.

Light says there will be little pressure to boost *Persona*'s commercial performance: "Her recordings are more important symbolically at this point, to show she hasn't left that world behind. She's never turned her back on hip-hop, but I think it's always been clear that she's not going to stay in just one place."

Or, he might add, rest on her laurels. "I've been in this business long enough that I've had great days and days when I'm over it," Latifah says. "But then someone will tell me their daughter was inspired by my being a big girl who's successful, or I'll meet a grown woman I inspired.

"The other morning I was (out shopping), and a lady told me how much I meant to her and to women of color, and women in general. When I hear that, I know that I'm doing the right thing, and that I should keep going."

—Elysa Gardner

Flawless: Queen Latifah (*far right*) poses with other celebrities during the Cover Girl 50th Anniversary Celebration in 2011. Latifah represented the company's makeup line for brown skin.

As she nurtured her own body, she realized that she was in a unique position to share with others what she knew about health, beauty, and self-love. She wanted people to see that "there is beauty in every kind of woman." She remembered that as a girl, she'd rarely seen women like herself—or products that truly served them—in the media. As a celebrity, she could finally do something about that. She began endorsing cosmetics that flattered brown skin and clothing that brought out the best in curvaceous bodies.

She also longed to share the many other lessons she'd learned throughout her life. "I wanted to say something to girls and women that would help them build their self-confidence and bring out their inner queens," she recalled. So she wrote another book. In *Put on Your Crown: Life-Changing Moments on the Path to Queendom* (2010), she described how key moments in her life shaped the person she has become. She encouraged readers to learn from her successes and failures.

Crowning moment: In 2010 Queen Latifah released another book titled *Put on Your Crown: Life-Changing Moments on the Path to Queendom.*

She was quick to point out that she still has a lot to learn and many goals she wants to achieve. "I'm not done yet," she insisted. "I will be a work in progress until the day I die."

GLOSSARY

apartheid: a set of laws effective in South Africa from 1948 to 1994. These laws separated whites from people of other races and limited the rights of nonwhites.

blues: a type of slow, sad music with roots in western Africa, invented by African Americans. The term *blues* means "sadness." The name of this music also comes from its use of "blue notes," or flat (slightly lowered) tones.

break: in hip-hop music, the brief part in a song during which the band drops out and the rhythm section takes over

civil rights movement: in the United States, a long series of nonviolent protests for racial equality. The movement began in 1955 with a bus boycott in Montgomery, Alabama, and ended in 1968 with the assassination of Martin Luther King Jr. This movement succeeded in changing U.S. laws to end legal racial discrimination.

credit history: a history of borrowing money and successfully repaying it

demo tape: a demonstration recording made on magnetic audiotape

discrimination: unfair treatment based on differences in race, age, gender, and other factors

down payment: a part of the full price paid at the time of purchase. The buyer pays the rest later.

flavor: in hip-hop slang, special

freestyling: in rap, improvising or making up a rap on the spot while performing

gangsta rap: rap music that portrays the violence and drug use of urban gang life in explicit language. Gangsta rap often expresses hostility toward white people, women, and authority figures.

hip-hop: the rhythmic dance music that usually accompanies rap, or rap together with this music

jazz: a type of music invented by African Americans that draws on blues, ragtime (dance music with a ragged, or syncopated, rhythm), and big-band orchestral music

minority: a part of a population differing from others in some characteristics, such as race or religion, and often treated unfairly

mixing: producing a sound recording by electronically combining or adjusting sounds from more than one source

mortgage: home loan

projects: a housing development planned, supported, and managed by government, usually for low-income families

racism: the belief that people of different races are inherently inferior or superior, or unfair treatment based on differences in race

rap: rhyming lyrics spoken or chanted over music

record: a vinyl disc with spiral grooves carrying recorded sound. The sound is encoded by fine variations in the edges of the grooves. A record-player needle placed in the grooves vibrates, reproducing the recorded sound, when the disc rotates at the correct speed.

reggae: a type of popular music that combines Jamaican music with elements of rock and soul

rhythm and blues (R & B): a type of popular music that blends blues and African American folk music. R & B usually has a strong beat and a simple structure.

riot: a tumultuous and/or violent disturbance of the public peace by three or more people acting together

rock and roll: blues-based music played with electric guitars, drums, and bass

scratching: the technique of moving a playing record back and forth rhythmically beneath the record-player needle

segregated: separated

sexism: the belief that one sex (usually female) is inherently inferior, or unfair treatment based on gender

soul: a type of music that mixes blues and black gospel music

stereotype: an oversimplified view or portrayal of a race, a gender, or a cultural group

SOURCE NOTES

6   Queen Latifah, *Ladies First* (New York: William Morrow and Co., 1999), 47–48.

7   Mickey Hess, ed., *Icons of Hip Hop* (Westport, CT: Greenwood Press, 2007), 218.

8   Latifah, *Ladies First*, xi.

10   Tom Gliatto and John Griffiths, "A Hit in *Living Single*, Queen Latifah Mourns the Loss of a Brother," *People*, November 29, 1993, 73.

10   Latifah, *Ladies First*, xviii.

10   Gliatto and Griffiths, "A Hit in *Living Single*," 74.

11   Latifah, *Ladies First*, xii.

11   Ibid., 40.

11   Queen Latifah, *Put on Your Crown* (New York: Hachette Book Group, 2010), 44.

12   Latifah, *Ladies First*, 38–39.

15   Lifetime Productions, *Intimate Portrait: Queen Latifah*, VHS (New York: Peter Leone Productions, 1996).

15   Latifah, *Ladies First*, 20.

17   Ibid., 16.

20   Ibid., 17.

20   Ibid., xiv–xv.

21   Ibid., 22.

21   Lifetime Productions, *Intimate Portrait*.

24   Latifah, *Ladies First*, 25.

24   Ibid., 28.

25   Ibid.

25   Latifah, *Put on Your Crown*, 86.

26   Latifah, *Ladies First*, 31.

28   Ibid., 30–31.

28   Lifetime Productions, *Intimate Portrait*.

28   Ibid.

28   Latifah, *Ladies First*, 42.

28   Ibid., 44.

31   Lifetime Productions, *Intimate Portrait*.
      Laurie Lanzen Harris, ed., "Queen Latifah," in *Biography Today* (Penobscot, MI: Omnigraphics, April 1992), 373.

32 White, "The Poet and the Rapper."

33 Latifah, *Ladies First*, 70.

33 Ibid., 69.

34 Ibid., 82.

34 Jeff Chang, *Can't Stop Won't Stop: A History of the Hip-Hop Generation* (New York: St. Martin's Press, 2005), 79.

36 Dennis Hunt, "Ten Questions: Queen Latifah," *Los Angeles Times*, September 8, 1991, 54.

37 Harris, "Queen Latifah," 373.

37 Carol Dekane Nagel, ed., *African American Biography* (New York: UXL, 1994), 605.

37 Keith Elliot Greenberg, *Rap* (Minneapolis: Lerner Publications Company, 1991), 30.

37 Harris, "Queen Latifah," 374.

38 Latifah, *Ladies First*, 55.

39 Aldore Collier, "A Royal Rap: Queen Latifah Reigns on and off TV," *Ebony*, December 1993, 118.

39 Latifah, *Ladies First*, 53–54.

39 Evelyn C. White, "The Poet and the Rapper," *Essence*, May 22, 1999, 122.

41 Latifah, *Ladies First*, 48–49.

41 Ibid., 58–59.

43 Ibid., 66.

43 Ibid., 64.

44 Lifetime Productions, *Intimate Portrait*.

44 Ibid.

44 Ibid.

45 Latifah, *Ladies First*, 62.

45 *Jet*, "Queen Latifah Says 'There's Life after *Living Single*,'" July 20, 1998, 38.

48 Latifah, *Ladies First*, 19.

48 Harris, "Queen Latifah," 373.

50 Hunt, "Ten Questions," 54.

50 Hunt, "Ten Questions," 54.

51 Latifah, *Ladies First*, 142–143.

52 Rock on the Net, "Queen Latifah," Rock on the Net, n.d., http://www .rockonthenet.com/artists-q/queenlatifah_main.htm (April 1, 2011).

53   Chris Dafoe, "Rapping Latifah Rules New Tribes," *Toronto Star*, May 18, 1990, D8.

54   Harris, "Queen Latifah," 374.
     White, "The Poet and the Rapper," 122.

54   Latifah, *Ladies First*, 68.

54   Ibid., 68–69.

54   Ibid., 70.

55   Tricia Rose, *Black Noise: Rap Music and the Black Culture in Contemporary America* (Middleton, CT: Wesleyan University Press, 1994), 165.

55   Nagel, *African American Biography*, 607.

56   Bobby Washington, *Who's Hot! Queen Latifah* (New York: Bantam Doubleday Dell, 1992), 39.

58   Nagel, *African American Biography*, 605.
     Cameron Barr, "Rap for the Masses," *Christian Science Monitor*, November 4, 1991, 10.

59   Deborah Gregory, "The Queen Rules," *Essence*, October 1993, 57.

60   Lifetime Productions, *Intimate Portrait*.

60   Harris, "Queen Latifah," 375.

60   Rock on the Net, "Queen Latifah."

60   Barr, "Rap for the Masses," 10.

60   Cheo Hodari Coker, "Queen Latifah Aims to Reign Over Films Too," *Los Angeles Times*, November 4, 1996, http://articles.latimes.com/1996-11-04/entertainment/ca-61091_1_queen-latifah/2 (April 5, 2011).

61   Latifah, *Put on Your Crown*, 79.

61   Ibid., 107.

61   Barr, "Rap for the Masses," 10.

64   Latifah, *Ladies First*, 78.

64   Collier, "A Royal Rap," 122.

65   Lynn Elber, "Queen Latifah Fights for Some Self-Satisfaction," *Toronto Sun*, May 19, 1994, 76.

66   Latifah, *Put on Your Crown*, 140.

66   Latifah, *Ladies First*, 88.

66   Ibid., 79.

66   Ibid., 105.

67   Latifah, *Put on Your Crown*, 146–147.

67   Ibid., 147.

67   Ibid.

70   Monika Guttman, "Queen's Troubled Reign," *USA Weekend*, November 6, 1994, 16.

71   Ibid.

71   *Jet*, "Queen Latifah Says She Is More Cautious after Being Carjacked," August 14, 1995, 59.

71   Ibid.

73   *Jet*, "Queen Latifah Says," 37.

75   Ibid., 38.

75   Stephen Holden, "*Set It Off* (1996): Just Trying to Get Even While They Get Rich," *New York Times*, November 6, 1996, http://movies.nytimes.com/movie/review?res=9F02E3D81338F935A35752C1A960958260 (April 10, 2011).

76   Jay Lustig and Carrie Stetler, "Latifah Is Queen of All She Does; Actress, Rapper, Manager Scores in Many Fields," *Minneapolis Star Tribune*, November 18, 1996, 7E.

76   *Jet*, "Queen Latifah Says," 35.

76   Ibid., 34.

78   Donna Freydkin, "When Latifah Reigns, She Pours It On," CNN.com, September 2, 1998, http://cgi.cnn.com/SHOWBIZ/Music/9809/02/queen
.latifah/index.html (April 11, 2011).

78   Charles Taylor, "Blue Romance," *Salon*, November 13, 1998, http://www.salon.com/entertainment/movies/reviews/1998/11/cov_13reviewb
.html (April 11, 2011).

78   *Jet*, "Queen Latifah Says," 35.

79   Ibid., 36.

79   Latifah, *Ladies First*, 2.

80   Kirkus Reviews, "Ladies First," *Kirkus Reviews*, December 1, 1998, http://www.kirkusreviews.com/book-reviews/non-fiction/queen-latifah/ladies-first/#review (April 11, 2011).

80   Lynn Norment, "Queen Latifah Has a New TV Show, a New Movie and New Sass," *Ebony*, November 1999, 117.

82   Ibid.

83   Ibid., 126.

85   Latifah, *Put on Your Crown*, 30.

85   Rebecca Ascher-Walsh, "Queen Victorious," EW.com, March 4, 2003, http://www.ew.com/ew/article/0,,422764,00.html (April 12, 2011).

88   Latifah, *Put on Your Crown*, 31.

88   Colin Devenish, "Queen Latifah Sings," *Rolling Stone*, September 28, 2004, http://www.rollingstone.com/music/news/queen-latifah-sings-20040928 (April 13, 2011).

88   Elizabeth Blair, "Queen Latifah Tunes into 'Trav'lin' Light,'" NPR, September 27, 2007, http://www.npr.org/templates/story/story .php?storyId=14747660 (April 13, 2011).

88   Mark Anthony Neal, "That's Ms. Owens to You!" *PopMatters*, November 11, 2004, http://www.popmatters.com/music/reviews/q/queenlatifah-danaowens.shtml (April 13, 2011).

89   William Ruhlmann, "Trav'lin' Light," Allmusic, September 25, 2007, http://www.allmusic.com/album/travlin-light-r1209611/review (April 13, 2011).

90   Latifah, *Put on Your Crown*, 80.

90   Ibid.

90   Ibid., 82–83.

91   Ken Capobianco, "'Persona' Lacks Queen's Attitude," Boston.com, August 24, 2009, http://articles.boston.com/2009-08-24/ ae/29256096_1_queen-latifah-persona-songs (April 13, 2011).

91   Andy Kellman, "Persona," Allmusic, July 7, 2009, http://www.allmusic .com/album/persona-r1591540/review (April 13, 2011).

91   Allison Stewart, "Quick Spin: Review of Queen Latifah's Album 'Persona,'" *Washington Post*, August 25, 2009, http://www .washingtonpost.com/wp-dyn/content/article/2009/08/24/ AR2009082402952.html (April 13, 2011).

91   Margaret Wappler, "Album Review: Queen Latifah's 'Persona,'" *Los Angeles Times*, August 24, 2009, http://latimesblogs.latimes.com/ music_blog/2009/08/album-review-queen-latifahs-persona.html (April 13, 2011).

91   Kellman, "Persona."

91   Latifah, *Put on Your Crown*, 30.

91   Ibid., 49.

91   Ibid., 53.

91   Ibid., 52–53.
94   Ibid., 55.
94   Ibid., 1.

SELECTED BIBLIOGRAPHY

Ascher-Walsh, Rebecca. "Queen Victorious." EW.com. March 4, 2003. http://
www.ew.com/ew/article/0,,422764,00.html (April 12, 2011).

Barr, Cameron. "Rap for the Masses." *Christian Science Monitor*, November 4,
1991, 10.

Blair, Elizabeth. "Queen Latifah Tunes into 'Trav'lin' Light.'" NPR. September
27, 2007. http://www.npr.org/templates/story/story
.php?storyId=14747660 (April 13, 2011).

Capobianco, Ken. "'Persona' Lacks Queen's Attitude." Boston.com. August 24,
2009. http://articles.boston.com/2009-08-24/ae/29256096_1_queen-
latifah-persona-songs (April 13, 2011).

Chang, Jeff. *Can't Stop Won't Stop: A History of the Hip-Hop Generation*. New
York: St. Martin's Press, 2005.

Coker, Cheo Hodari. "Queen Latifah Aims to Reign Over Films Too." *Los
Angeles Times*, November 4, 1996. http://articles.latimes.com/1996-11-
04/entertainment/ca-61091_1_queen-latifah/2 (April 5, 2011).

Collier, Aldore. "A Royal Rap: Queen Latifah Reigns on and off TV." *Ebony*,
December 1993, 118.

Dafoe, Chris. "Rapping Latifah Rules New Tribes." *Toronto Star*, May 18, 1990,
D8.

Devenish, Colin. "Queen Latifah Sings." *Rolling Stone*, September 28,
2004. http://www.rollingstone.com/music/news/queen-latifah-
sings-20040928 (April 13, 2011).

Elber, Lynn. "Queen Latifah Fights for Some Self-Satisfaction." *Toronto Sun*,
May 19, 1994, 76.

Freydkin, Donna. "When Latifah Reigns, She Pours It On." CNN.com.
September 2, 1998. http://cgi.cnn.com/SHOWBIZ/Music/9809/02/queen
.latifah/index.html (April 11, 2011).

Gliatto, Tom, and John Griffiths. "A Hit in *Living Single*, Queen Latifah Mourns
the Loss of a Brother." *People*, November 29, 1993, 73.

Greenberg, Keith Elliot. *Rap*. Minneapolis: Lerner Publications Company,
1991.

Gregory, Deborah. "The Queen Rules." *Essence*, October 1993, 57.

Guttman, Monika. "Queen's Troubled Reign." *USA Weekend*, November 6, 1994, 16.

Harris, Laurie Lanzen, ed. "Queen Latifah." In *Biography Today*. Penobscot, MI: Omnigraphics, April 1992.

Hess, Mickey, ed. *Icons of Hip Hop*. Westport, CT: Greenwood Press, 2007.

Holden, Stephen. "*Set It Off* (1996): Just Trying to Get Even While They Get Rich." *New York Times*. November 6, 1996. http://movies.nytimes.com/movie/review?res=9F02E3D81338F935A35752C1A960958260 (April 10, 2011).

Hunt, Dennis. "Ten Questions: Queen Latifah." *Los Angeles Times*, September 8, 1991, 54.

Jet, "Queen Latifah Says She Is More Cautious after Being Carjacked." August 14, 1995, 59.

——."Queen Latifah Says 'There's Life after *Living Single*.'" July 20, 1998, 38.

Kellman, Andy. "Persona." Allmusic. July 7, 2009. http://www.allmusic.com/album/persona-r1591540/review (April 13, 2011).

Kirkus Reviews. "Ladies First." *Kirkus Reviews*. December 1, 1998. http://www.kirkusreviews.com/book-reviews/non-fiction/queen-latifah/ladies-first/#review (April 11, 2011).

Latifah, Queen. *Ladies First*. New York: William Morrow and Co., 1999.

——. *Put on Your Crown*. New York: Hachette Book Group, 2010.

Lifetime Productions. *Intimate Portrait: Queen Latifah*. VHS. New York: Peter Leone Productions, 1996.

Lustig, Jay, and Carrie Stetler. "Latifah Is Queen of All She Does; Actress, Rapper, Manager Scores in Many Fields." *Minneapolis Star Tribune*, November 18, 1996, 7E.

Nagel, Carol Dekane, ed. *African American Biography*. New York: UXL, 1994.

Neal, Mark Anthony. "That's Ms. Owens to You!" *PopMatters*. November 11, 2004. http://www.popmatters.com/music/reviews/q/queenlatifah-danaowens.shtml (April 13, 2011).

Norment, Lynn. "Queen Latifah Has a New TV Show, a New Movie and New Sass." *Ebony*, November 1999, 117.

Rock on the Net. "Queen Latifah." Rock on the Net. N.d. http://www.rockonthenet.com/artists-q/queenlatifah_main.htm (April 1, 2011).

Rose, Tricia. *Black Noise: Rap Music and the Black Culture in Contemporary America*. Middleton, CT: Wesleyan University Press, 1994.

Ruhlmann, William. "Trav'lin' Light." Allmusic. September 25, 2007. http://www.allmusic.com/album/travlin-light-r1209611/review (April 13, 2011).

Schoemer, Karen. "Six Nights for Sampling a World of Unsung Bands." *New York Times*, July 13, 1990. http://query.nytimes.com/gst/fullpage.html?res=9C0CE1D91539F930A25754C0A966958260 (April 3, 2011).

Stewart, Allison. "Quick Spin: Review of Queen Latifah's Album 'Persona.'" *Washington Post*. August 25, 2009. http://www.washingtonpost.com/wp-dyn/content/article/2009/08/24/AR2009082402952.html (April 13, 2011).

Taylor, Charles. "Blue Romance." *Salon*. November 13, 1998. http://www.salon.com/entertainment/movies/reviews/1998/11/cov_13reviewb.html (April 11, 2011).

Wappler, Margaret. "Album Review: Queen Latifah's 'Persona.'" *Los Angeles Times*. August 24, 2009. http://latimesblogs.latimes.com/music_blog/2009/08/album-review-queen-latifahs-persona.html (April 13, 2011).

Washington, Bobby. *Who's Hot! Queen Latifah*. New York: Bantam Doubleday Dell, 1992.

White, Evelyn C. "The Poet and the Rapper." *Essence*, May 22, 1999, 122.

FURTHER READING AND WEBSITES

Books

Anderson, Adrienne. *Word: Rap, Politics and Feminism*. Lincoln, NE: Writers Club Press, 2003.

Bloom, Sarah R. *Queen Latifah*. New York: Chelsea House, 2001.

Galens, Judy. *Queen Latifah*. Farmington Hills, MI: Lucent Books, 2007.

Herr, Melody. *Sitting for Equal Service: Lunch Counter Sit-ins, United States, 1960s*. Minneapolis: Twenty-First Century Books, 2011.

Kallwn, Stuart A. *Open the Jail Doors—We Want to Enter: The Defiance Campaign against Apartheid Laws, South Africa, 1952*. Minneapolis: Twenty-First Century Books, 2011.

Koestler-Grack, Rachel A. *Queen Latifah*. New York: Infobase Publishing, 2007.

Latifah, Queen. *Ladies First*. New York: William Morrow and Co., 1999.

———. *Put on Your Crown*. New York: Hachette Book Group, 2010.

Lindop, Edmund. *America in the 1960s*. Minneapolis: Twenty-First Century Books, 2010.

Madden, Annette. *In Her Footsteps: 101 Remarkable Black Women from the Queen of Sheba to Queen Latifah*. San Francisco: Conari Press, 2000.

Richards, Marlee. *America in the 1970s*. Minneapolis: Twenty-First Century Books, 2010.

Snyder, Gail. *Queen Latifah*. Broomall, PA: Mason Crest Publishers, 2007.

Websites

Allmusic: Queen Latifah
http://www.allmusic.com/artist/queen-latifah-p96755
This website is a one-stop shop for information on Queen Latifah's music. Visitors will find a biography, a discography, a complete song list, an outline of chart positions, and awards for each album and song. The site is also loaded with sound recordings, videos, and links to related artists.

The Birth of Rap: A Look Back
http://www.npr.org/templates/story/story.php?storyId=7550286
Visitors to this site can listen to several radio stories and interviews celebrating the history of hip-hop music.

Can't Stop Won't Stop

> http://cantstopwontstop.com
> On this website, Jeff Chang, author of *Can't Stop Won't Stop: A History of the Hip-Hop Generation*, offers excerpts from his book, a blog, and news from the hip-hop world.

The Lancelot H. Owens Scholarship Foundation

> http://www.lhosf.org
> The home page of Flavor Unit Entertainment's charitable division provides information on the foundation's activities and instructions for requesting its help.

Newark Riots 1967

> http://www.67riots.rutgers.edu/n_events.htm
> This website, sponsored by New Jersey's Rutgers University, explores in detail the events, people, and places affected by the 1967 riots in Newark.

Old School Hip Hop

> http://www.oldschoolhiphop.com
> Visitors to this site will find a wealth of information on the pioneers of hip-hop.

Queen Latifah

> http://www.queenlatifah.com/pages/home
> The official site of Queen Latifah offers news and tour information; a biography, discography, and filmography; and multimedia galleries including photos, music, music videos, and film clips.

Queen Latifah Biography

> http://www.biography.com/articles/Queen-Latifah-9542419
> This site offers a full video biography of Queen Latifah in six parts.

PHOTO ACKNOWLEDGMENTS

The images in this book are used with the permission of: © Jon McKee/CORBIS, p. 1; © Dan MacMedan/USA TODAY, pp. 3, 6; © Bettmann/CORBIS, p. 4; © Al Pereira/ Michael Ochs Archives/Getty Images, pp. 5, 43, 47; © Barry Winiker/Photolibrary, p. 8; © Gregg DeGuire/WireImage/Getty Images, p. 9; © Latitudestock/Gallo Images/ Getty Images, p. 12; Mary Evans/Everett Collection, p. 13; Everett Collection, pp. 14, 74, 77, 81; AP Photo, pp. 16, 23; © Adem Demir/Shutterstock Images, p. 17; National Archives, p. 18 (photo no. 306-SS-28B-35-6); © Burt Shavitz/Time & Life Images/ Getty Images, p. 19; © Ron Galella, Ltd./WireImage/Getty Images, p. 21; Newark Public Library, p. 22; © Michael Ochs Archives/Getty Images, pp. 25, 38, 40, 45; © Dan Steinberg/Getty Images, p. 27; AP Photo/Mike Derer, p. 30; © Hulton Archive/Getty Images, p. 32; © HCIR/Globe Photos, Inc., p. 33; © Vinnie Zuffante/Archive Photos/ Getty Images, p. 34; © Jemal Countess/WireImage/Getty Images, p. 35; © Frank Micelotta/Getty Images, p. 36; © Raymond Boyd/Michael Ochs Archives/Getty Images, p. 41; © DocsHollywood ETV/Globe Photos, Inc., p. 42; © Catherine McGann/Hulton Archive/Getty Images, p. 44; © Tory Zimmerman/USA TODAY, pp. 46, 49, 62, 69, 72 (top), 82, 92; © LGI Stock/CORBIS, p. 48; Tommy Boy Records, p. 51; Jeffrey Davy/ Rex Features USA, p. 52; © Neal Preston/CORBIS, p. 53; © Jeff Kravitz/FilmMagic, Inc/ Getty Images, p. 57; AP Photo/Paul Drinkwater/NBCU Photo Bank, p. 59; © Gary Moss/ CORBIS, p. 61; © Tim Mosenfelder/Getty Images, pp. 63, 75; © Bill Davila/Retna Ltd., p. 64; Warner Brothers/courtesy Everett Collection, p. 68; © Jim Smeal/WireImage/ Getty Images, p. 71; © New York Daily News Archive/Getty Images, p. 72 (bottom); © Tom Rodriguez/Globe Photos, Inc., p. 78; © Walter Weissman/Globe Photos, Inc., p. 79; © Reuters/CORBIS, p. 83; Miramax/The Kobal Collection, p. 84; © SGranitz/ WireImage/Getty Images, p. 85; New Line/The Kobal Collection/James, David, p. 86; Jim Smeal/BEImages/Rex Features USA, p. 87; © Timothy A. Clary/AFP/Getty Images, p. 89; © Billy Tompkins/Retna Ltd., p. 90; © John Shearer/Getty Images, p. 94; Picture Perfect/Rex Features USA, p. 95.

Front cover: © Paul Zimmerman/Getty Images.

Back cover: © Dan MacMedan/USA TODAY.

Main body text set in USA TODAY Roman Regular 10.5/15.

ABOUT THE AUTHOR

Amy Ruth Allen has written six biographies for Lerner Publishing Group, Inc. She lives in central Virginia with her husband, Leigh, and is currently working on a young adult novel.